DRESSMAKING MADE EASY

Made Easy Series

DRESSMAKING MADE EASY

BY
ISABEL DE NYSE CONOVER

Wildside Press

INTRODUCTION

It is the object of this book to set forth the quickest and best method for every operation, in sewing. It is a handy book of reference, where the making of any part of a garment can be easily looked up.

The making of a whole garment may seem a difficult proposition but, when thought of in individual parts, it resolves itself into simple operations. It is merely a series of joining seams, turning edges for hems, and sewing pieces together for pockets and other trimmings. Any woman who can run a sewing machine can join the pieces, if she knows how to place the goods and where to stitch.

The things which have often seemed intricate in the methods of the experienced tailor and dressmaker are shown as they really are — simple means of procedure in sewing followed out step by step. Every question in the making of a garment is anticipated and answered, from the cutting out of the pieces to the sewing on of the last hook and eye. In some cases there are other ways of accomplishing the same or a similar result, but by actual and repeated tests the methods advocated in this book have proven the most satisfactory. It is based on years of experience in manufacturing patterns and making garments.

CONTENTS

DRESSMAKING MADE EASY

CHAPTER I

PREPARING THE MATERIAL AND CUTTING

To Shrink Woolens or Cottons in Woolen Finish. — Spread out the material on a smooth surface and cover it with a wet cloth. Unbleached muslin or an old sheet doubled makes an excellent shrink cloth.

Dip the shrink cloth in clean cold water. Do not wring it dry. Squeeze out only part of the water and place the cloth on the material dripping wet. After the wrinkles have been smoothed out of both the fabric and the shrink cloth, roll the fabric and its wet covering over a flat thin board. The wet cloth should be long enough to wrap several times around the outside of the fabric. Slow drying shrinks the material. After twelve hours unwrap the material and press while damp. To

[9]

avoid shining the surface, press on the wrong side or cover the material with a cloth.

Goods with selvedge should have the selvedge cut off before shrinking. The weave of the selvedge being different from the fabric may cause the selvedge to shrink more or less than the goods, making puckers along the edge.

Woolens or cottons in woolen finish which are not shrunk before they are made will water spot and shrink unevenly when exposed to moisture. It is impossible to press properly unshrunk fabrics of this description. When the material is dampened and a hot iron applied, the steam will shrink it in spots and may spoil the fit of the garment.

To Shrink Wash Fabrics. — Soak the material in clean cold water and hang it in a shady place to dry or roll in a Turkish towel. It is slow drying that shrinks the goods. Press the material before it is entirely dry. It is important to shrink wash fabrics before making up. All cottons, linens and raw silks shrink when tubbed.

If the fabric is colored, put the proper ingredient in the water to set the shade.

To Set Blue, Brown or Brownish Red Shades. — Soak the material for two hours in sugar of lead water. Use one ounce of sugar of lead to every gallon of water. Allow the sugar of lead to dissolve thoroughly before placing the material in the water. This process will set the above mentioned colors permanently.

To Set Green, Mauve, Purple or Purplish Red Shades. — Soak the material in alum water for ten minutes. The proper solution is one ounce of alum to one gallon of water.

Proper Tools. — *An electric motor* attached to an ordinary sewing machine will double its capacity.

Heavy shears cut a clean edge which is easy to follow in sewing. Cut with the points of the shears resting on the table.

An accurate tape measure is essential. A misfit is often due to the wrong size of pattern ordered according to an incorrect tape measure. To test the tape, stretch it along a wooden ruler and determine if it is correctly marked.

A *tracing wheel* makes a distinct mark easily followed in stitching if the material is of firm texture. It is an excellent means of indicating the position of pleats, tucks, hems, etc.

Steel pins do not mar the fabric like lead ones. If the pins have black heads they are easy to see and to pick up.

Laying the Pattern on the Goods. — If all the pattern pieces are laid on the goods before any one piece is cut, they can be shifted around and placed to the best advantage. It saves material to plan the arrangement of the pieces instead of cutting haphazard one piece at a time. There are two ways of placing the pattern pieces on the goods or making a layout. One method is to spread the material in a single thickness and lay on each piece of the pattern twice, once for the right and once for the left side of the garment, and another way is to double the goods and lay on each pattern piece only once.

If the material is spread in a single thickness

place it face down on a smooth surface and arrange the pattern pieces on the wrong side of the goods, fitting them in to the best advantage. Place the large pieces on first and fill in with the small pieces.

Lay each pattern piece on twice, marking it in first for one side, then reversing it by turning it over for the other side. To avoid cutting two pieces for one side mark an X on the side of each pattern piece which corresponds to the left side of the finished garment, considering that the piece will be placed on the wrong side of the goods. Lay the pattern on the goods with the X marks showing and mark around each piece. This provides for the left side of the garment. Turn the pieces over and mark around them for the right side, in which case none of the X marks will show. Where both right and left sides of the garment are cut in one piece, as in the case of a one-piece back, lay the center-back edge of the pattern straight of the goods. Mark around all edges of the pattern except the center-back. Turn the pattern over, keeping the center-back on the same thread of the material, and mark around all edges again except center-back.

The closest possible layout can be made when the material is spread in a single thickness. The pieces can be interlocked and large and small pieces worked in alongside of each other. For instance, the material may not be wide enough to cut two waist fronts, while a sleeve and front will just take the width.

If the material is doubled crease it through the center bringing the face sides of the goods together and lay it on a smooth surface. Lay all the pattern pieces on, placing the large pieces on first. In this case, each pattern piece is laid on only once. As the material is double, two pieces are cut at the same time. Where the right and the left sides are to be cut in one piece, as a one-piece back, lay the center-back edge of the pattern on the fold of the material.

If the material has an up and down, as some figured goods and fabric with nap, lay all the pattern pieces one way. Place the pattern so the top of each piece heads in the same direction.

To Match Plaids. — Mark off the seam allowance on the pattern pieces. This gives the exact sewing line. After the pieces are laid on the goods, mark where the lines of the plaid will come on the sewing line. Shift the pieces until the lines of the plaid come at exactly the same place on the sewing line in pieces which join together. It is impossible to match plaids with the seams on the pattern. The lines of the plaid may match at the outer edges and not come anywhere near meeting at the sewing line.

Marking Around the Pattern and Indicating the Perforations. — After determining the proper position of the pieces weight them down, using ordinary paper weights or books. A pattern cannot be pinned to the material without dragging the material out of shape. Mark around the outside edges of the pattern with wax or chalk.

If the material has sufficient body so the marks will not show through on to the right

[15]

side, wax or chalk mark the perforations for hems, pleats, etc. Lay the pieces for the two sides of the garment together. Place the pattern in position and mark perforations with the wax or chalk. Remove the pattern. Pass a pin through the two thicknesses of the material at each perforation. Turn the pieces over and wax or chalk mark the under piece at each pin.

Awl marking is one means of indicating perforations in materials having firm texture. Before removing the pattern from the goods place the point of the awl center way of the perforation and, with the awl in a perpendicular position, bear sufficient weight on it to make a hole in the goods.

Thread marking is used in delicate fabrics or materials of loose texture which will not hold the awl mark. Use thread which contrasts in color to the material. Lay corresponding pieces together, that is, the right and the left fronts together, etc. Where the right and the left sides are cut in one, as in the case of a one-piece back, fold the piece through the center. Place the pattern in position and pass the needle perpendicularly through the perforation in the pattern and the two thicknesses of the goods, bring it up through the perforation and repeat two or three times, keeping the stitches loose. Remove the pattern and pass the scissors between the two thicknesses of the goods clipping the threads. If the stitches have been taken sufficiently loose, the thread will be long enough to hold in the goods.

Cutting. — *Use heavy shears,* keep the points on the table and always cut away from you. It is impossible to follow a line accurately when the wrist is bent.

Cut just inside the lines which outlined the pattern. Since the pattern itself was inside these lines they should be cut off. Cut accurately. An eighth of an inch added in one place and a quarter of an inch in another may come at the same place in joining and spoil the fit.

Mark notches by slashing the goods for a depth of a quarter of an inch at each notch.

[17]

This is better than cutting a notch as the slash is not so apt to fray.

To cut a true bias fold the material diagonally, bringing a crosswise thread to a lengthwise thread. Cut along the diagonal line. See Fig. 1.

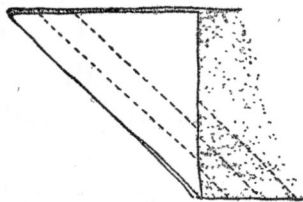

FIG. 1

Pressing. — Woolens and cottons in woolen or cotton finish should be covered with a damp cloth when pressed. Heavy muslin is the best fabric for a press cloth. Keep a basin of water handy and dip the press cloth in this, wringing it only partly dry.

Under pressing simplifies sewing. Press each piece after it is cut and each seam after it is stitched. Hems, tucks, etc., are more easily and neatly stitched if they are pressed into position first. Press collars, cuffs and other trimming before attaching them to the garment.

To steam out slight ease or fulness in woolen

materials, cover with a wet cloth and press with a hot iron. Run a gather thread in the material and draw it up the desired amount, cover the material with a wet cloth and press with a hot iron. Bring the iron down squarely on the goods, rest it a second, then remove it, permitting the material to steam. Repeat the process.

To remove shine on the surface of woolens caused by a too hot iron or wearing, steam the goods. Cover the goods with a wet cloth and press with a hot iron. Rest the iron and raise it alternately to steam the goods. While the goods is steaming brush it with a stiff whisk brush.

CHAPTER II

HAND SEWING

Running Stitch. — This is the simplest of hand stitches. It is used in plain sewing, basting, blind stitching and for various other purposes. To form a running stitch, insert the needle in the goods, pass it along the under side and bring it out on the surface again. See Fig. 2.

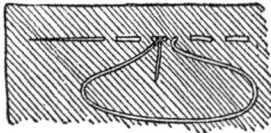

FIG. 2

Back Stitch. — Where a firm stitch is desired for joining two pieces or a stay is wanted for running stitches, a back stitch is taken. To form a back stitch take a running stitch; then insert the needle at the point where it was first put in to form the running stitch. See Fig. 3. This makes a back stitch.

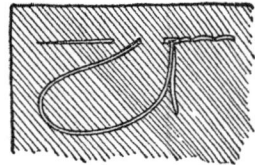

FIG. 3

Basting. — *Long and short stitch* is the type of basting used to hold seams and for attaching trimming. Take a long running stitch and a short running stitch and repeat three times; then take a back stitch. Always use a cotton which contrasts in color. It is easily seen and removed.

In basting seams take a scant seam allowance. When stitching take the exact seam allowance which will bring the stitching to one side of the basting. If stitched in this manner the basting thread is easily removed, but should the stitching come on top of the basting it is impossible to remove the basting thread without breaking the thread of the stitching.

When basting before pressing use fine silk. It does not leave an imprint like a coarse cotton.

Zigzag basting is used to hold interlinings in place. Take stitches crosswise of the material, inserting the needle each time directly below the place where it was first put in the goods. See Fig. 4. Zigzag basting holds the material more firmly than long and short stitches.

Felling.—This stitch is used in hemming, sewing in linings, etc. Thumb tack the ma-

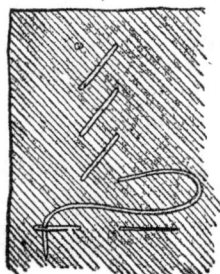

FIG. 4

terial securely to the top of the sewing table and work toward you. Insert the needle diagonally in the surface of the upper fabric and take a short stitch. Bring the needle out through the surface of the under fabric and re-peat, being careful that the stitches do not show through on the right side of the goods. See Fig. 5.

Blind Stitching. — Where two pieces of material are to be caught loosely together blind stitching is used. Bring the needle out

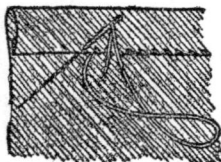

FIG. 5

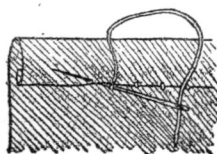

FIG. 6

through the upper piece and insert it directly below in the under piece, being careful that it does not show through on the right side of the goods. Continue taking these stitches at regular intervals. See Fig. 6.

Overcasting. — To keep a raw edge from fraying whip it with over and over stitches. Insert the needle on the under side of the piece, bring it out on the outside and repeat at regular intervals. See Fig. 7.

Padding Stitch. — Padding stitch is used in coat making to hold canvas interlinings in

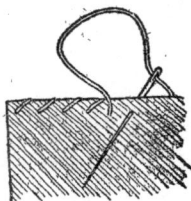

FIG. 7

place. Pin the canvas in place and hold the garment canvas side toward you. Take a stitch crosswise of the material, passing the needle through the canvas and the material, but using care that the stitch does not show through on the right side of the goods. Make the stitch not over one quarter of an inch in length. Insert the needle directly below the first point of inserting and take a cross stitch as before. Repeat the stitches in

[23]

parallel rows, reversing the slant of the between stitches and bringing the cross stitches
in each alternate row cen-
ter way between the cross
stitches of the first row. See
Fig. 8. In working on
revers or collars roll and
shape the revers or collars
into the position they are to
take on the finished garment.

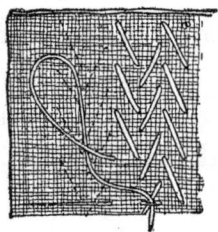

FIG. 8

Buttonholes. — *To space buttonholes evenly*,
determine where the top and bottom buttonholes will be placed and divide the space
between by one less than the number of buttonholes. For instance, if there are six buttonholes to be placed in a space of five inches,
divide five inches by five and it gives one inch
which is the distance between buttonholes.

To work a plain buttonhole mark the exact
length of the buttonhole. Cut along the mark
making a clean slash. Sew along the slash
by hand, taking running stitches so that the
material will not stretch. Start at the inside
end of the slash and take the first stitch.

Work from the right side of the goods. Secure the thread on the wrong side near the end of the buttonhole and bring the needle and thread out through the slash onto the right side of the material. Insert the needle through the slash onto the wrong side and bring the point out on the right side of the goods, one sixteenth of an inch above the

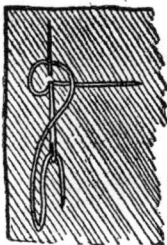

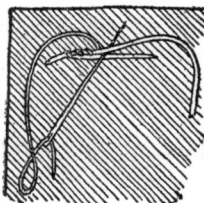

FIG. 9   FIG. 10

slash. Pass the thread over the back of the needle and under the point. See Fig. 9. Draw the needle through the goods and repeat the stitch until the buttonhole is worked across the top, around the front end, and across the bottom. Secure end of buttonhole with over and over stitches. Use button twist in making buttonholes in woolens or silk and coarse cotton thread on cotton goods.

[25]

To pad buttonhole whip a cotton cord to the edge. See Fig. 10. When the stitches are worked over this, the buttonhole will give a heavy ridged appearance. Padding the buttonhole also strengthens it.

Rounded end buttonholes are made in heavy fabrics where the buttons are large, as they give added space for passing the button through the buttonhole. To make a rounded end buttonhole, mark the slash on the material, lay the material on a smooth surface and cut the slash with a sharp knife. At the front end of the buttonhole cut out a circle of material about an eighth of an inch across. See Fig. 11. Use the point of the knife to cut out the circle, being careful not to stretch the buttonhole. Rounded end buttonholes are usually padded. Use the regulation buttonhole stitch in working the buttonhole.

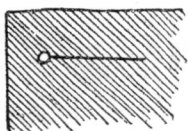

FIG. 11

To prevent buttonholes from puckering in sheer fabrics such as chiffon, place a drop of melted paraffin wax on the wrong side of the

[26]

material in the exact spot where the button-hole is to be worked. Smooth the wax down and work the buttonhole as usual. When finished place a piece of Manila paper on the wrong side of the goods and press with a hot iron. The buttonhole will be perfectly smooth and all trace of the paraffin wax gone.

Sewing on Buttons. — *To mark position of buttons* lap buttonholes over button stand in finished position. Chalk or pencil mark under material through buttonholes. This gives exact position of buttons.

Dress and underwear buttons are sewed flat on the material. Place pins in two holes of

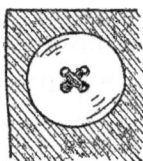
Fig. 12

Fig. 13

Fig. 14

the buttons to keep it in position. Use a thin needle and strong thread. In a four-holed button the stitches may be crossed in the center, Fig. 12, worked in two bars, Fig. 13,

or worked in what is called a crow's foot,
Fig. 14. After taking seven or eight stitches
in each hole bring the needle out between the
button and goods. Wrap the thread around
the button several times. Pass the needle
through onto the wrong side of the goods and
secure the thread with several over and over
stitches.

To sew buttons on thin materials, such as
chiffon, baste lawn to the under side of the
material. In sewing on the button take the
stitches through the chiffon and the lawn, cutting the lawn away close to the button after
it is sewed in place. If desired, tape may be
used in place of the lawn.

Coat buttons are raised from the material.
To do this place a match across the button
and work the stitches over the match. Remove the match after working seven or eight
stitches. Pass the needle between the button
and material. Pull the button out so the
stitches are taut and wrap the thread between
the button and material until the button
stands up stiffly. Then pass the needle onto

the wrong side of the goods and fasten the thread with several over and over stitches.

Tailor's Tacks. — Where a stay is needed at the corner of a pocket or at the end of a dart a tailor's tack is made. These vary in form.

Bar tacks are made by taking four or five over and over stitches about one quarter of

Fig. 15

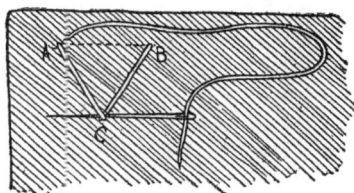

Fig. 16

an inch in length, then covering these with over and over stitches worked close together. See Fig. 15.

Arrowheads are made in the shape of a triangle. See Fig. 16. Bring the needle up at point *A* and take a short stitch at point *C*. See Fig. 16 for position of needle. Insert the needle at point *B* and bring it out on the upper line of the triangle just to the side of

[29]

the first stitch. Take a stitch at the bottom
of the triangle just above the first stitch and
insert the needle on the upper line, near point
B and next to the last stitch. Bring it out on
the upper line near point *A* and close to the
first stitch. Repeat until the triangle is com-
pletely covered.

CHAPTER III

SEAMS AND THEIR USES

Open Seams. — When the seam is stitched only once and the raw edges are pressed apart, it is called an open seam. This is used in medium and heavy weight materials where a flat finish is desired, as in the seams of skirts or the underarm and shoulder joinings of woolen dresses. To form an open seam, lay the two pieces of the material with the right or face side of the goods together and stitch, taking the exact seam allowance. Press the seams open. See Fig. 17.

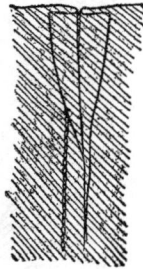

FIG. 17

The edges of the seam can be finished with overcasting, pinking or binding. See *Overcasting*, page 23.

Pinking is formed by cutting small triangular shaped notches in the edge. Edges cut in this manner do not fray as readily as a straight edge.

If *binding* is used, bind the edge of each piece separately before joining. See *Binding*, page 113.

French Seams. — A French seam has the edges doubled in so no raw edges show. This type of seam is used on blouses, wash dresses, infants' clothes and lingerie.

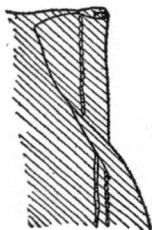

Fig. 18

To form a French seam lay the two pieces of the material to be joined with the wrong sides of the material together and stitch the length of the seam, running the stitching one eighth of an inch from the edge. Turn the pieces wrong side out and crease along the stitching. Stitch again the length of the seam, running the stitching one quarter of an inch from the creased edge. See Fig. 18. This takes the regulation seam allowance of three eighths of an inch. If more or less is allowed for the seam, make the stitchings correspondingly farther or nearer to the edge.

[32]

Double Stitched Seams. — If a second stitching is placed just back from the joining, the seam is called a double stitched seam. Coat and skirt seams are often double stitched for trimming. Lay the two pieces to be joined with the right sides of the material together and stitch the length of the seam, running the stitching in a seam's width. If the garment is unlined overcast the raw edges, see *Overcasting*, page 23, or bind the raw edges, inserting both raw edges in the one binding. See *Binding*, page 113. Turn both edges toward the side where the second

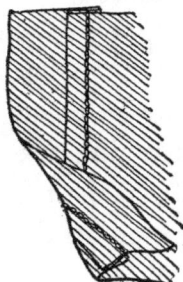

FIG. 19

stitching is to be placed. Baste, press and stitch the length of the seam, stitching on the right side of the garment. See Fig. 19. The second stitching is usually placed from one eighth to one quarter of an inch from the seam. If the stitching is placed the exact width of the machine foot from the seam the foot can be used as a gage in stitching.

Lap Felled Seams. — When both edges of the seam are turned under and the seam is stitched flat, it is called lap felled. Men's shirts and underwear and women's tailored blouses are made in this manner. Lay the two pieces to be joined with the wrong sides together. Place the under piece so it extends one quarter of an inch beyond the upper piece. Stitch the length of the seam running the stitching one quarter of an inch from the edge of the upper piece. See Fig. 20. Open up the two pieces and crease along the joining. Turn under the free edge and stitch it flat over the upper piece. See Fig. 21. This makes a seam allowance of three eighths of an inch. If the seam allowance varies, place the first stitching correspondingly nearer or farther from the edge.

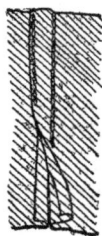

FIG. 20

FIG. 21

Slot Seam. — When the seam is under faced it is called a slot seam. Seams of this

[34]

type are used for trimming purposes in medium weight materials. Fold under the seam allowance on both pieces to be joined and press the edges. Cut a strip of material a half inch wider than twice the seam allowance. Bind both edges of this piece. See *Binding*, page 113. Mark the center of the strip with chalk or a tracing wheel.

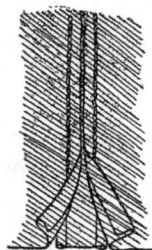

FIG. 22

Place the two pieces to be joined on top of the strip of material, bringing the folded edge of each piece to the center of the strip. Pin or baste in position and stitch the length of the seam twice, running the stitchings one quarter of an inch back from the folded edge of each piece. See Fig. 22.

Hemstitched Seams. — Where a light effect is desired in ladies' blouses, children's cotton dresses and lingerie the seams are hemstitched. Lay the two pieces to be joined with the right sides together and stitch the length of the seams, running the stitching a seam's width back from the edge. Fold both raw edges back one way, baste in place and press. Have the garment machine hemstitched over the exact joining. Cut away the raw edges close to the hemstitching. See *Hemstitching with an Ordinary Sewing Machine,* page 115.

Seam Beading. — Tape embroidered to simulate hemstitching is called seam beading. This gives an effect similar to hemstitching and is used on underwear and infants' garments. Cut off all but one eighth of an inch seam allowance on the pieces to be joined. French seam one edge of the seam beading to one piece and French seam the edge of the beading which is free to the other piece. Make the French seam not more than one eighth of an inch wide when finished. It takes three sixteenths of an inch allowance to make a French seam one eighth of an inch wide. With only one eighth of an inch seam allowance the pieces would be short if joined directly together. However, the seam beading coming between adds the extra amount, making the size correct. If the seam beading is wider than one eighth of an inch finished, cut off proportionally more from the pieces to be joined.

CHAPTER IV

TUCKS, PLEATS AND FULLNESS

Pin Tucks. — The narrowest tuck that can be made is called a pin tuck. They are used as a trimming in sheer fabrics.

To form a pin tuck crease the material, bringing the wrong sides together and stitch about one sixteenth of an inch from the creased edge. Where it is possible, pin tuck the material before cutting the garment out. If the piece is pin tucked after it is cut, more or less may be taken up than is allowed for, making the garment consequently small or large. See *How to Use a Block Waist Pattern*, page 118.

Side Tucks. — If any portion of a garment is caught together with stitching, making a fold of goods, and the fold turned to one side and pressed flat, it forms a side tuck. Side tucks are used as trimming in thin and medium weight materials. They vary in width.

To form a side tuck crease the material along the line which will be the free edge of the tuck, bringing the wrong sides of the material together. Press the crease and mark the stitching line with chalk or wax or use a sewing machine foot with a gage in stitching. Stitch through the two thicknesses of the material, plac-

FIG. 23

ing the stitching the width of the tuck back from the edge. See Fig. 23. Fold the tuck into the finished position and press.

To make a gage for spacing a group of tucks cut a straight piece of cardboard and notch the cardboard at the outer edge and sewing

FIG. 24

line of each tuck as they will appear when finished. Cut the lower edge of the notch at right angles to the edge of the cardboard and the upper edge of the notch diagonally. See Fig. 24.

Side Pleats. — Where material is lapped over to take out fullness it forms a side pleat. Side pleats are used in the

[39]

top of skirts, bloomers, etc., where fullness is desired but where bulkiness is to be avoided.

To form a side pleat determine the amount of material to be taken up in the pleat. Mark this space on the right side of the goods, placing the first mark at the fold of the pleat. Bring the two marks together forming the pleat. See Fig. 25.

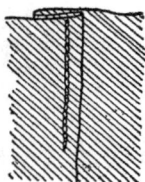

FIG. 25

Soft pleats are pleats which are unstitched. They are used in pliable materials.

In *stitched side pleats* the needle passes through the three thicknesses of the material. The stitching is placed any desired distance from the fold.

Box Pleats. — A box pleat is two side pleats turned away from each other. These are used as trimming on waists, skirts and children's dresses. Determine the amount of material to be taken up in the pleat. Mark the amount on the material and fold the goods center way on the marks, bringing the wrong sides of the goods together. Stitch the

[40]

finished width of the pleat back from the edge of the fold, which will be along the marks. Open up the material, bring the fold center way over the stitching and press. If desired stitch down either side of the pleat. See Fig. 26.

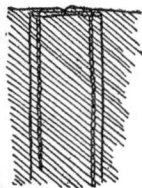

FIG. 26

Double Box Pleats. — Where side pleats are added either side of a box pleat and turned away from the box pleat, it is called a double box pleat. The effect is of one box pleat on top of another. This type of pleat is used in children's dresses and ladies' skirts.

Simulated Box Pleats. — If two side pleats are turned away from each other with a space between, they form a simulated box pleat. It does not take as much material as a box pleat but gives the same appearance. Determine where the center of the simulated box pleat is to be. Measure out half the width of the simulated box pleat at either side and fold under shallow side pleats. See Fig. 27.

[41]

Inverted Box Pleat. — When two side pleats are turned toward each other and the edges of the two pleats meet, they form an inverted box pleat. These are used in skirts and children's dresses. To form an inverted box pleat first determine the amount of material

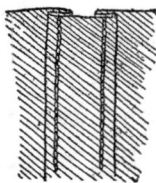

Fig. 27

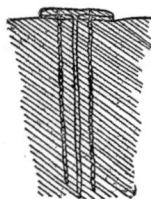

Fig. 28

to be taken up in the pleat. Mark the amount on the material to be pleated and place another mark center way of the space. Crease the material along the outside lines and bring these folded edges to the center line. See Fig. 28. It is a matter of choice whether or not the pleat is stitched. If the pleat is stitched, run the stitching parallel to the creased edges and back any desired amount from the edges.

Plain Shirring. — Where the material is gathered in parallel rows it forms plain

shirring. Shirring is used as trimming in
thin goods or to regulate the hang of fullness
in heavy materials. Make a cardboard gage
to space shirring. See Fig. 24. Mark the
lines where the shirring is to be placed. Run
the shirr strings in by hand, taking running
stitches and using
a fine needle and
fine thread knotted
at the end. See
Fig. 29. After the
shirring has been

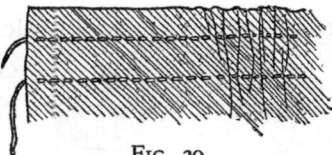

FIG. 29

drawn up the proper amount, fasten the
shirr string securely with over and over
stitches.

To reinforce shirring, baste lawn to the
wrong side of the material along the lines of
shirring after the shirring has been drawn up.
Machine stitch over the lines of shirring or
secure the lawn to the material with back
stitches worked by hand. See *Back stitch,*
page 20. After the lawn is fastened to the
goods cut it away between the lines of
shirring.

Tuck Shirring. — When a small tuck is taken up on each line of shirring it is called tuck shirring. This particular trimming is suitable only for sheer goods. To form tuck shirring, crease along each line of shirring, bringing the wrong sides of the material together. In running in the shirr strings, place the stitches back a little way from the creased edges. Spacing the shirr string back an eighth or a quarter of an inch from the edge gives a good effect.

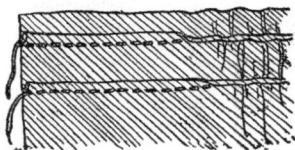

FIG. 30

When the shirr strings are drawn up, there is a tuck or heading formed on each line of shirring. See Fig. 30. Tuck shirring may be reinforced as described on page 43.

Cord Shirring. — If the material is gathered up on a cord at each line of shirring, it forms a cord shirring. Cord shirring makes attractive trimming in medium weight as well as sheer goods. To form cord shirring, crease the material as for a tuck shirring, inserting a cotton cord along the crease, taking the stitches just in back of the cord and shirring the material up on the cord. See Fig. 31.

If a sewing machine is equipped with a one-sided foot, the cord can be stitched in by machine. Place the material in the machine so the cord comes on the side of the needle which is not covered with the foot. After the stitching is finished shirr the material up on the cord.

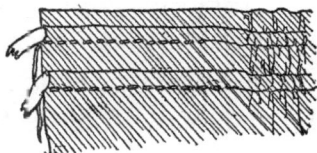

Fig. 31

The cotton cord used for cord shirring is called cable cord. It comes in various sizes.

To Keep Shirring Equally Distributed. — Divide the material to be shirred into four equal parts and use separate shirr strings for each part.

CHAPTER V

CLOSINGS AND PLACKETS

Closings with Hems. — When there is an allowance of material beyond the finished edge of the closing and it is turned back onto the wrong side of the garment, it forms a hem.

Unstitched hems are held with buttons and buttonholes. Before folding under the hems, bind the raw edges, see *Binding*, page 113, or turn off a seam's width on each raw edge, stitch the length of the hems running the stitchings one eighth of an inch from the edges. Then turn under the hems, creasing along the finished edges of the closing, work buttonholes in one hem and sew buttons to the other. See Fig. 32.

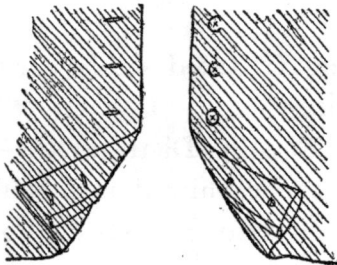

FIG. 32

Stitched hems are formed in the same way, except that they are stitched the hem's width back from the edge or felled by hand. See *Felling*, page 22.

Facings and Extensions. — Where there is only a seam allowance at the closing and the appearance of a hem is desired, finish the right side of the opening with a facing and the left side with an extension. Decide how deeply the closing is to lap. Cut the facing the width of the lap, allowing seams extra. Face the right side. See *Facing*, page 92.

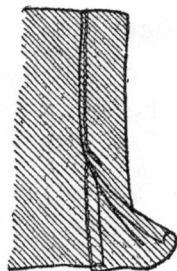

FIG. 33

Lay the extension with the right side next to the wrong side of the material, and stitch the length of the closing, running the stitching a seam's width in from the edge. Turn under the free edge of the extension a seam's width, fold the extension through the center, press and stitch the free edge of the extension over the raw edges. See Fig. 33. In closing, the right side, which

[47]

is the faced side, laps over the left side and hides the extension.

Blind Closings. — Where the buttons and buttonholes, hooks and eyes or snaps are hidden the closing is called a blind closing. Whether the closing is finished with hems or a facing and extension, it can be made a blind closing by adding an underlap to the right-hand side.

As the underlap will be double, cut it twice the width of the finished hem or facing, allowing seams extra. Fold the underlap through the center, press and work buttonholes or sew on hooks or snaps. Cut the seam allowance off the back edge of the hem or facing to make the closing less bulky. After the hem is turned back onto the wrong side, or the facing stitched to the edge of the garment and turned back, insert the raw edges of the underlap under the free edges of the hem or facing. See Fig. 34. Baste the length of the

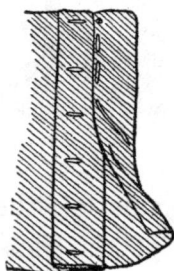

FIG. 34

[48]

closing. Turn the underlap back onto the hem. Press, baste and stitch through the underlap, the hem, the turned under edges of the underlap and the outside garment. Run the stitching the length of closing, stitching the width of the hem or facing back from the edge. See Fig. 35.

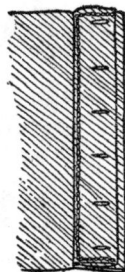

FIG. 35

Closing Under Tucks. — When the tuck comes at a seam, bind the raw edge of the tuck before stitching the tuck in place, see *Binding*, page 113, and face the portion of the material which extends under the tuck. See *Facing*, page 92.

If the tuck comes midway of a piece and there is to be a closing under the tuck for a certain depth, slash the material under the tuck for the desired depth, placing the slash a seam's width beyond the stitching of the tuck. See Fig. 36. Bind the raw edge of the tuck before stitching. Finish the under edge of the opening with a facing. Lay the facing

[49]

with the right side of the facing next to the right side of the material and stitch the length

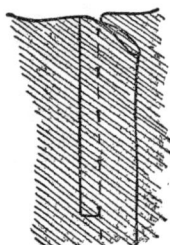

Fig. 36

of the closing, running the stitching a seam's width in from the edge. Let the facing extend beyond the material far enough to reach the stitching of the tuck. Then fold the facing onto the wrong side. Turn under the free edge of the facing a seam's width and stitch the facing to the wrong side of the garment, placing the stitching so it will come just under the edge of the tuck when the tuck is brought over into the finished position. See Fig. 37. At the bottom of the closing fasten the facing to the under side of the tuck with over and over stitches.

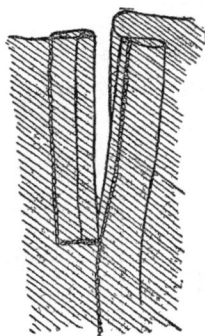

Fig. 37

Box Pleat Closings. — A box pleat closing is one having a box pleat on the top edge of the closing. The under edge of the closing is usually finished with a hem or facing.

To form the box pleat on the edge of a closing turn under the raw edge a seam's width. Determine the amount of material to be taken up in the box pleat. Mark this space on the material, measuring in from the seam. Bring the edge with the seam turned off to this mark. Work-

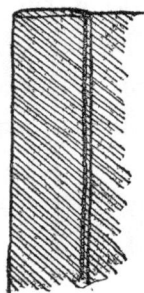

Fig. 38

ing from the wrong side of the garment, stitch the length of the closing. See Fig. 38. Flatten the loop of material thus formed by placing the center of the loop over the line of stitching. Press and run a stitching either side of the pleat. See Fig. 39. Stitching placed from an eighth to a quarter of an inch from the edge gives a good effect.

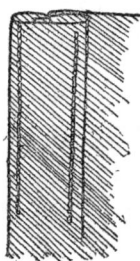

Fig. 39

Simulated Box Pleat Closings.— These give the same appearance as a box pleat closing but to avoid having the seam at

[51]

the center of the pleat the raw edge is thrown to one side. Form the simulated box pleat along the edge of the material, then lay on the pattern and cut the piece. In the case of a blouse bring the center-front of the blouse pattern to the center of the pleat.

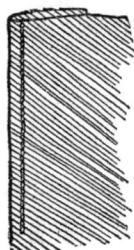

FIG. 40

To form a simulated box pleat two inches wide, measure in from the edge of the material two inches and make a mark at the top and bottom of the piece. Measure two inches beyond these first marks and mark again at top and bottom. Crease the material along the first marks, bringing the wrong sides of the material together. Press and stitch the length of the piece, running the stitching from an eighth to a quarter of an inch back from the edge. See Fig. 40. Crease along the second line of marks, bringing the wrong side of the material on top of the portion folded under in the first creasing. Press the edge and stitch from top to bottom of the piece, running the stitching

[52]

the same distance from the edge that the first stitching was placed from the edge. This stitching will be through three thicknesses of material. See Fig. 41. The effect is similar to a box pleat. See Fig. 42. If a wider or narrower pleat is desired, vary the spacing of the fold lines correspondingly.

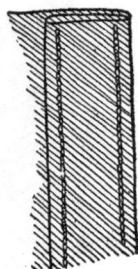

FIG. 41

Applied Box Pleat Closings. — If an extra piece of material is added at the closing to give the appearance of a box pleat, the closing is called an applied box pleat closing.

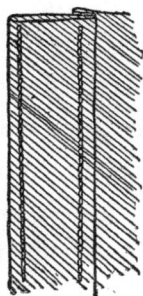

FIG. 42

To form an applied box pleat closing two inches wide, cut a straight piece of material three and one quarter inches wide. Lay the strip along the edge of the material with the right side of the strip next to the wrong side of the garment. Stitch the length of the piece, running the stitching the regulation seam allowance — three eighths

[53]

of an inch from edge. Crease the strip of material one quarter of an inch beyond the joining, folding it along this creased line onto the right side of the piece. Stitch one quarter inch from this edge. Fold under the raw edge, press and stitch it flat to the goods, running the stitching one quarter of an inch in from the edge. See Fig. 43. Lay on pattern and cut after pleat is formed.

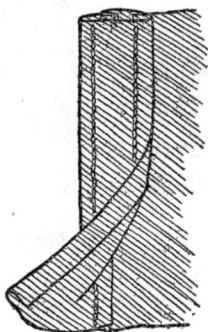

FIG. 43

Closings at Shoulder, Armhole and Underarm. — Closings of this description should be finished with shaped facings and extensions. To cut the facing and extension so they will exactly fit, use the front body pattern as a guide. A facing or extension of this type should measure about three quarters of an inch wide, finished, and be cut one and one half inches wide to allow for seams. Measure back one and a half inches from shoulder, armhole and underarm edges on front body

[54]

pattern. Lay the pattern on another piece of paper. Mark around the outside edges at the neck, shoulder and underarm and run a tracing wheel over the marks which were placed one and one half inches back from the edge. Remove the pattern and cut out the piece thus marked. This gives a pattern for the facing and extension. Cut one piece for a facing and two pieces for an extension. Join the facing to the front of the garment at the shoulder, armhole and underarm. See *Facing*, page 92.

Lay the two pieces for the extension with the right sides together, and stitch around the outside edges, taking the regulation seam allowance — three eighths of an inch. To avoid bulkiness cut off the seam close to the stitching. Slash the raw edges at the corner and turn the extension right side out. Turn in free edges of the extension a seam's width, and press. Insert the raw edges of the back shoulder, the sleeve and the back underarm between the two thicknesses of the extension. Stitch around the closing, running the stitching on the extension, and stitching through the two pieces of the extension and the inserted edges of the back and sleeve.

Slash Closings with Pleats Below. — Infants' dresses are often finished with a slash at the center-back and pleats below. To allow for such a closing the center-back of

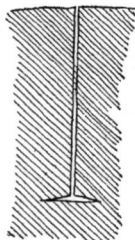 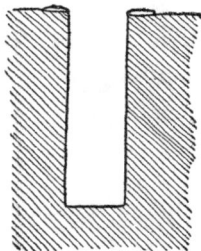 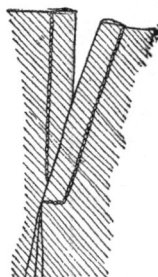

FIG. 44   FIG. 45   FIG. 46

the pattern must be laid one inch from the fold of the material. Slash the fold the desired depth and cut crosswise slashes at the bottom three quarters of an inch wide. See Fig. 44. Turn a hem either side of the lengthwise slash, creasing the material three quarters of an inch from the raw edges. See Fig. 45. Turn under the raw edge one quarter of an inch and machine stitch or fell

the hem by hand. See *Felling*, page 22.
The hems will be one half inch wide, finished.
Lap the right hem over the left hem, and lay
the material at the bottom of
the slash into small pleats.
See Fig. 46. Tack these folds
securely in place with over
and over stitches on the wrong
side of the garment. See Fig.
47.

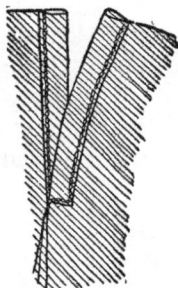

FIG. 47

Continuous Facings.—When
both sides of a vent are finished
with a strip of material, it is called a continuous facing. This finish is used for vents
in drawers and petticoats and on plackets in
children's dresses and ladies' skirts where
there is fullness at the waist line.

For a continuous facing that is to finish
three quarters of an inch wide, cut the material two and one quarter inches wide and one
half inch longer than twice the depth of the
placket.

If it is a slash that is to be finished with
the continuous facing, place the right side of

the facing next to the wrong side of the material, and with the edge of the facing even with the edge of the material at the top but with the facing extending nearly a seam's width beyond the edge of the slash at the bottom. Stitch down one side of the slash and up the other, keeping the stitching a seam's width in from the edge of the facing.

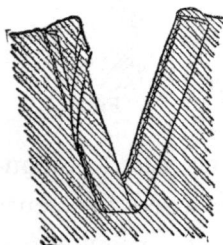

The seam taken on the slashed edge will narrow to almost nothing at the bottom of the slash. Turn under the free edge of the facing three eighths of an inch, fold the facing through the center and stitch the free edge over the raw edge on the right side. See Fig. 48.

FIG. 48

If the placket comes at the joining of two pieces, close the seam below the placket. At the bottom of the placket slash the raw edges to the depth of the seam. Take several over and over stitches to keep the seam from ripping below the placket. In placing the facing

[58]

on the goods, keep the edges even at the top and bottom, and take the regulation seam allowance at all points.

Skirt Plackets. — *In gathered skirts* the placket is usually finished with a continuous facing.

Plackets on plain seams in fitted skirts have a facing on one side and an extension on the other. Unless reversed for trimming purposes, the right side of the placket laps over the left and is faced.

Use the skirt pattern as a guide in cutting the facing. Mark the depth of the placket on the skirt gore which comes to the right of the placket. Measure back from the edge of the pattern two and three quarter inches and draw a line at this point from top of skirt to a seam's width below placket. Lay the pattern on another piece of paper. Mark the outline at the top and side, and run a tracing wheel over the line which is two and three quarter inches back from the edge. Use this pattern as a guide in cutting the facing.

[59]

In woolens or cottons which stretch easily, tape the edge of the skirt at the right of the placket. Lay the tape on the wrong side of the material a seam's width in from the edge. See *Taping*, page 130. After the tape is caught to the material, turn the raw edge of the seam onto the tape and tack it in place. Press, and sew on the hooks, keeping them slightly in back of the edge. Turn under the back and bottom edges of the facing a seam's width, press and stitch along

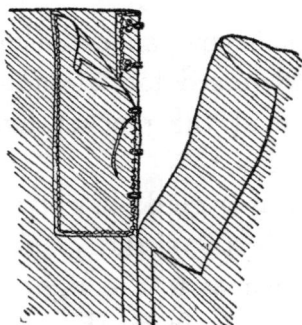

FIG. 49

the folded edges. Turn under the front edge of the facing a seam's width and fell the front edge to the skirt along the placket. See Fig. 49. Baste the facing across the top to the top of the skirt.

If the left side of the placket has the extension cut on it, as some skirt patterns are made, face this extension with material cut the same shape as the outside. Turn under the seam allowance at the back edge of the facing and stitch along the edge. Place the facing on top of the extension with the right side of the facing next to the right side of the extension, and stitch at the side and across the bottom. To avoid bulkiness, cut the seam off diagonally at the corner. Turn the facing onto the wrong side of the skirt. Baste the facing to the skirt at the top, and press.

At the bottom of the closing catch the facing

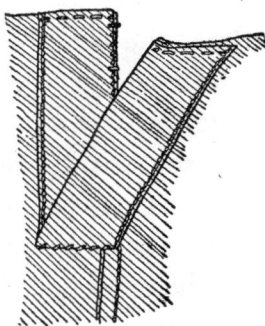

Fig. 50

on the right hand side of the closing to the extension on the left. Use over and over stitches. Sew eyes to the extension to match hooks on the right side of the skirt. See Fig. 50.

If there is no extension cut on the left side of the skirt, use the facing pattern as a guide to cut two extension pieces. Lay the two extension pieces with the right sides together and stitch across the sides and bottom. To avoid bulkiness, cut off the seams diagonally at the corners. Turn right side out, turn in the free side edges a seam's width and press. Insert the raw edge of the skirt between the two edges of the extension, and stitch the length of the placket. Lap the right side over the left as described before.

Plackets at center-front have an underlap and the seam below the placket is pressed open. Cut the material for the underlap three and three quarters inches wide and one half inch longer than the depth of placket. The lining for the underlap should be the same shape. Lay the lining on the right side of the underlap and stitch down the sides and across the bottom, running the stitching a seam's width from the edge. To avoid bulkiness cut off the seam diagonally at the corners. Turn the underlap right side out. Turn under raw edges a seam's width and press. Stitch around the outside again to make the underlap firmer. Face right side of skirt at placket as described in *Plackets on Plain Seams*, page 59.

Place center of underlap a seam's width from left edge of placket with the right side of the underlap next to the right side of the skirt. Working from the wrong side of the skirt, stitch from top to bottom of the placket, running the stitching a seam's width in from the raw edge of the placket. Turn the underlap onto the wrong side of the skirt. Catch the lower edge of the underlap to the skirt, using care that the stitches do not show through onto the right side of the goods. See Fig. 51.

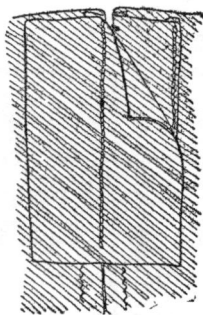

FIG. 51

The Fly on Boys' Trousers. — *Trousers with drop seat* have a small fly in front and the seam closed above. In stitching the front and crotch seam leave a space, three and one half inches, open at the lower front. Use the front trousers pattern as a guide in cutting the facing and fly pieces. These should be crescent-shaped. Indicate the points on the pattern where the seam is left open. Centerway between these points measure back on the pattern three inches. Draw a half circle touching the point three inches back from the edge and the points where the seam is open. Lay the pattern on another piece of material, make the outline of the crotch seam and go over the half circle with a tracing wheel. Remove the pattern and add a seam beyond the half circle. This gives a pattern for both fly and facing. Cut three pieces, two for the fly which is sewed to the right side of the trousers and one piece for facing the left side of the trousers.

Bind the outer edges of the facing piece. See *Binding*, page 113. The left front of the trousers is faced across the opening. Lay the facing piece on the face side of the material. Be sure that it is placed so the curve of the crotch seam matches in the facing piece and the trousers. Stitch the facing to the trousers, running the stitching a seam's width in from the edge across the opening. Turn the facing onto the wrong side and fell in place at outer edges. See *Felling*, page 22.

Lay the two pieces for the fly with the right sides of the material together. Stitch around the outer edges, running the stitching a seam's width in from the edge and turn right side out. Press the fly and lay on top of the front of the trousers which comes to the right of the opening, matching edges. Stitch the under edge of the fly to the trousers across the opening, running the stitching a seam's width in from

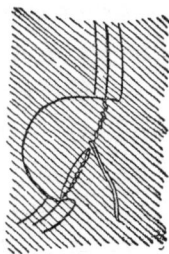

FIG. 52

the edge. Turn the fly inside the trousers, turn under the free edge of the fly a seam's width and hand fell it in place. See Fig. 52.

Open-front trousers have a fly from top to crotch. In this case the crotch seam is closed only from the top in back to the leg seam, the front of the trousers being finished on the right side with a long fly and on the left side with a facing. Use front trousers

pattern as a guide in cutting the fly and facing. Mark a point on the pattern two and
one half inches in from the top of the crotch
seam. Continue down the seam, marking
points at this depth until the curved portion
at the crotch is reached. Here narrow in
the line and round it off. Lay the pattern on
another piece of paper, mark the outline at
the crotch seam and run a tracing wheel
over the pencil marks. Remove the pattern
and add seams at the back edge of the piece.
Use this pattern as a guide in cutting the
facing, fly and underlap for buttonholes.
One piece is needed for the facing, two for
the fly and two for the underlap. Use a
firm thin lining material for the underlap.

Bind the back edge of the facing. Lay
the facing on the face side of the left trouser
front, matching the raw edges. Stitch the
facing to the trousers, running the stitching a
seam's width in from the raw edge. Turn
the facing onto the wrong side, press and
baste into position.

Lay the two pieces for the underlap with

the right sides together. Stitch along the outside edge. Turn the underlap right side out. Turn under the free edges a seam's width, baste and press. Work buttonholes and baste underlap to left side of trousers, placing it on top of the facing and with the edge just in back of the edge of the trousers. From the wrong side of the trousers, stitch the underlap and facing to the outside of the trousers, running the stitching along the back edge of the underlap. Catch the underlap to the facing between each buttonhole with over and over stitches.

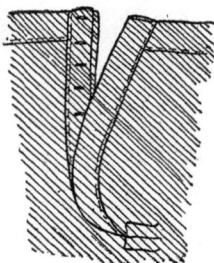

FIG. 53

Stitch the fly and attach it in the same manner as *the fly in the drop-seat trousers.* See Fig. 53.

The Front of Men's Underdrawers. — Underdrawers are made to lap at the top. There is material allowed beyond the center front on each side. Close the crotch seam as described in *boys' open front trousers* and face both sides of the front opening. Use

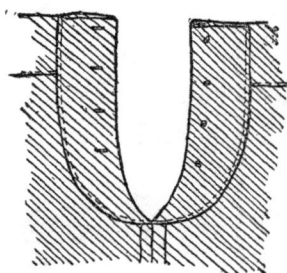

FIG. 54

the front drawers pattern as a guide in cutting the facing. See *open front boys' trousers* for cutting facing and sewing it on. After the fronts are faced, lap the drawers, bringing the center fronts together. The drawers will lap deepest at the top, running to nothing at the crotch. Fasten with buttons and buttonholes. See Fig. 54.

CHAPTER VI

POCKETS

Patch Pockets. — This type of pocket is formed by applying a piece of material on top of the garment.

Cut the pocket any desired shape and line it. See *Lining Trimming Pieces*, page 95. Fell or machine stitch the pocket to the garment. See Fig. 55.

Slash Pockets. — Where the material is slashed and pocket pieces sewed underneath, it is called a *plain slash pocket*.

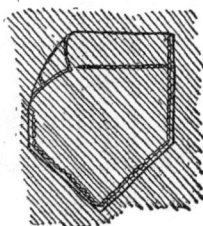

Fig. 55

To make a plain slash pocket mark the position of the slash on the material. Cut two pocket pieces one inch longer than the slash and any desired width, rounding off the bottom. Lay one pocket piece so it extends above the mark, lapping it only a seam's

width over the mark.　　Stitch the pocket
piece to the material, running the stitching
just above the slash mark and parallel to it.
See Fig. 56.　Place the other pocket piece

FIG. 56

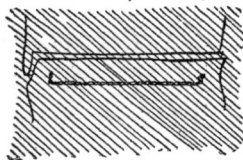

FIG. 57

below the slash mark with a seam's width
extending above it.　Stitch this piece to the
material, running the stitching parallel to
the slash mark and just below.　The two
stitchings should be not over one eighth of
an inch apart.　At the ends of the slash mark,
run stitchings on the lower piece at right

FIG. 58

angles to the first stitching and
from the stitching in the lower
to the stitching in the upper
pocket piece.　See Fig. 57.　Stitch back
and forth two or three times to make it
firm.　Slash centerway between the two
stitchings and diagonally to the corners.　See

[70]

Fig. 58. Turn the two pocket pieces through the slash onto the wrong side of the garment. Baste the edges of the slash together, press and stitch around the slash again for trimming. The two pocket pieces will lie on top of each other on the wrong side of the garment. Stitch the two pocket pieces together, running

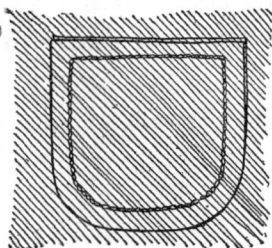

FIG. 59

the stitching a seam's width from the edges. See Fig. 59. If the garment is unlined, bind the raw edges of the pocket pieces. See *Binding*, page 113. Stay the ends of the pocket on the right side of the garment with

FIG. 60

tailor's tacks. See Fig. 60 and *Tailor's Tacks*, page 29.

To make a *slash pocket with flap* proceed as for a *plain slash pocket*, inserting the flap between the garment and the pocket piece at the top of the slash. Do not cut slash until pieces are attached.

Line the flap, leaving the top edges raw.
See *Lining Trimming Pieces*, page 95. In
placing the upper pocket piece, put the flap
under it with the right side of the flap next
to the right side of the garment and the bottom
of the flap lapping a seam's width over the
slash mark. Stitch the upper and lower
pocket pieces in place as in a *plain slash
pocket*. When the pocket
pieces are turned through
the slash onto the wrong
side of the garment the
flap remains on the right
side. Fig. 61. Turn the
raw edges at the top of
the slash up onto the
garment and from the right side of the
garment stitch just above the flap, running
the stitching the length of the slash. Stitch
the inside pocket pieces as described in making a *plain slash pocket*.

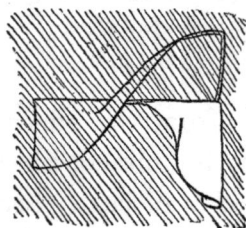

FIG. 61

A *welt pocket* is a form of slash pocket which
has an inset piece of material at the bottom
of the slash. This inset piece of material is

[72]

called the welt. Welt pockets are used in waistcoats and coats.

To make a welt pocket, mark where the finish welt is to come on the garment. A welt three quarters of an inch wide gives a good appearance. Then mark centerway between the upper and lower edges of the welt to within one half inch of either end. From the end of the center line mark diagonal lines to the corners of the welt. See Fig. 62. These center lines are where the material will be slashed. Cut two pocket pieces to

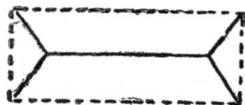

FIG. 62

extend a seam's width beyond the welt marks on either side. The pocket piece which is to be sewed to the lower edge of the slash should be cut the width of the finished welt longer than the pocket piece which is to be sewed to the upper edge of the slash. Place the pocket pieces on the right side of the material with the edges just meeting at the center line on the welt. Stitch across the pocket pieces, running the stitching equal

[73]

distances from the slash mark and placing the two rows at a distance apart which just

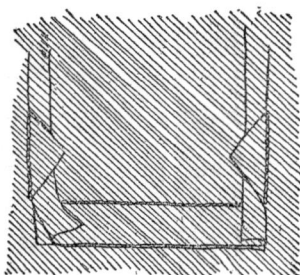

FIG. 63

equals the width of the finished welt. Slash on mark centerway between the stitchings and diagonally at the corners. Turn the pocket pieces through the slash onto the wrong side. Turn both pocket pieces up above the slash and stitch the lower pocket piece to the material at the ends of the slash. See Fig. 63.

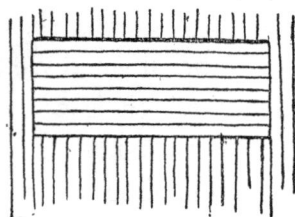

FIG. 64

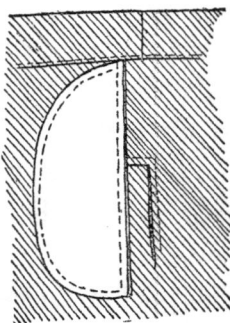

FIG. 65

Turn the two pocket pieces so they hang down and stitch around the outside edges.

On the outside the welt will appear as in Fig. 64.

Boys' Trousers Pockets. — Face the front trousers at the pocket for a space of two inches. See *Facing*, page 92. The back of boys' trousers are cut with an extension at the pocket. Cut two inside pocket pieces and join the top of one to the facing and the top of the other to the extension. Stitch the two pieces together at the outer edges. See Fig. 65.

CHAPTER VII

SLEEVES AND HOW TO HANG THEM

Sleeve Vents. — Shirt sleeves have a vent at the back finished with a pointed top facing. Divide the bottom of the sleeve in half and then divide the back half in half again. This will give the point where the sleeve should be slashed for the vent. Usually the slash is about four inches deep.

Finish the back edge with an extension. Cut a straight piece of material one and three quarter inches wide and a seam's width longer than the slash. Turn off a seam at the top and press the edge. Lay this extension along the back edge of the slash. Keep the edges even at the bottom but place the edge of the extension nearly a seam's width beyond the slash at the top. Stitch the length of the slash, running the stitching a seam's width in from the edge of the extension piece. On the edge of the slash there will be a seam taken at the bottom running to nothing at the top of the slash. Turn under the free edge of the extension a seam's width, fold the extension through the center and stitch it flat over the raw edges on the wrong side of the sleeve.

Cut a pointed facing for the front edge of the slash which will finish one inch wide. Mark a line on a piece of plain paper four inches long as line *AB* in Fig. 66. One inch beyond this line mark another line parallel to it, as line *CD* in Fig. 66. Draw a cross line at the top between points *A* and *C* and mark the center of it, lettering this point *E*. Mark a point one and one quarter inches above *E*, lettering it *F*. From this point draw diagonal lines to points *A* and *C*. Mark another line, as *GH*, one half inch beyond line *CD* and parallel to it. Continue the line *AC* until it reaches line *G*. At the bottom draw a straight line across, touching points *B*, *D*, and *H*. Add the regulation seam allowance

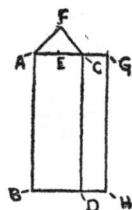

FIG. 66

at all points. This gives a pattern for the pointed facing.

Turn under the top and the side edges *AB* of the facing a seam's width and press. Lay the facing on the wrong side of the sleeve with the right side of the facing next to the wrong side of the material and the edge *GH* next to the edge of the slash. Place the facing so the edges match at the bottom but with the edge of the facing extending a seam's width beyond the slash at the top. Stitch the length of the slash, running the stitching a seam's width from the edge of the facing. Fold the facing along line *CD*, bringing the pointed portion onto the right side of the sleeve. The point should come directly over the slash. Stitch the facing flat to the sleeve, running the stitching near the edge. Stitch across what was line *CA* on the pattern, which will catch the extension at the back of the slash securely to the upper facing. See Fig. 67.

FIG. 67

[78]

Short slashes in blouse sleeves are finished with continuous facings. See *Continuous Facings*, page 57.

Cuffs. — Band cuffs on shirt sleeves are sewed on after the sleeve seam is closed. Lay the cuff lining on the cuff with the right sides of the material together. Stitch across the ends and the bottom of the cuff. Cut off the corners diagonally near to the stitching and turn the cuff right side out. Place the cuff on top of the sleeve, with the wrong side of the cuff next to the wrong side of the sleeve, the raw edges of the cuff even with the bottom

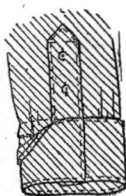

FIG. 68

of the sleeve and the ends of the cuff coming to the end of the facing and extension at the vent in the sleeve. Stitch the inside cuff to the sleeve, leaving outer cuff free. Turn the cuff down into the finished position. Turn under the free edge of the cuff a seam's width and fell it over the raw edges on the right side of the sleeve (see *Felling*, page 22), or stitch it down by machine. See Fig. 68.

[79]

Band cuffs on sleeves without vents are sewed to the sleeves before the sleeve seams are joined. Join the lining to bottom of the cuff, with the raw edges of the seam extending on the wrong side of the pieces. Leave the ends of the cuff and lining free. Join the cuff to the bottom of the sleeve with the raw edges of the seam extending on the inside of the sleeve. See Fig. 69. Then join the sleeve seam, the ends of the cuff and cuff lining in one continuous stitching. Turn the cuff lining onto the wrong side of the sleeve, fold in the free edge and fell it over the raw edges at the joining of the cuff and sleeve.

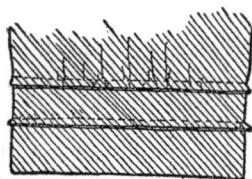

FIG. 69

French cuffs are double cuffs which do not lap, but are held together at the end with cuff links. These are used on shirt sleeves which have a vent.

If a stiff cuff is desired interline with coarse lawn, carrying out the plan outlines in interlining *Detachable Collars*, page 98. After

the interlining is pinned in place, lay the two
pieces for the cuff with the right sides of the
material together and stitch
across the bottom and the ends,
leaving the edge which will
fasten to the sleeve free. Cut
off the seams near the stitching
to avoid bulkiness, turn the cuff
right side out and press. Lay
the cuff on top of the sleeve

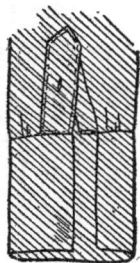

FIG. 70

with the raw edges of the cuff along the
bottom of the sleeve. Bring one end of
the cuff to the end of the facing on the
front of the vent, but bring the other end
of the cuff only to the joining of
the extension and sleeve. See
Fig. 70. In stitching, join one
thickness of the cuff to the lower
edge of the sleeve. Turn the cuff
down, fold in the free edge and
fell it over the raw edges at the
joining of the cuff and sleeve.

FIG. 71

Fold the cuff through the center, turning
the lower section back on the upper. Work

[81]

buttonholes in the end and fasten with cuff links. See Fig. 71.

Turn back cuffs on sleeves without vents give the best appearance when they are sewed on after the sleeve seams are closed. If the cuffs are lined, join the lining to the top of the cuff with the raw edges of the seam extending on the wrong side of the pieces. Open up the cuff and lining, and join the ends with the seams extending on the wrong side. Turn the sleeve wrong side out and slip the cuff over the sleeve with the right side of the cuff next to the wrong side of the sleeve and the bottom of the cuff even with the bottom of the sleeve. Stitch the cuff to the sleeve, running the stitching around the bottom of the sleeve and leaving the cuff lining free. Turn the sleeve right side out and the cuff into the finished position, folding under the free edge of the lining a seam's width, and felling it down by hand or stitching it by machine. See Fig. 72.

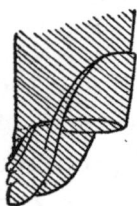

Fig. 72

[82]

Unlined turn-back cuffs are usually sewed to the sleeve after the sleeve and cuff seams are joined. In this case, French seam the joining in the cuff. See *French Seams*, page 32. Turn the sleeve wrong side out and slip the cuff over the sleeve bringing the right side of the cuff next to the wrong side of the sleeve, and the lower edges even. Stitch around the bottom of the sleeve. Turn the sleeve right side out and the cuff into the finished position.

To Measure a Sleeve. — Mark off the seam allowance on the top and sides of the sleeve pattern. Pin the shoulder seams of the pattern and mark off the seams at the armhole and underarm. Measure around the armhole and across the top of the sleeve with the edge of the tape. A sleeve should be at least an inch and a half larger than the armhole.

To Make a Sleeve Smaller at the Top. — Lay in a dart tuck at the center of the sleeve pattern running from the top to the bottom. Crease the pattern lengthwise through the center, bringing the side edges together. At the top of the sleeve pattern mark half the width of the tuck on either side of the crease.

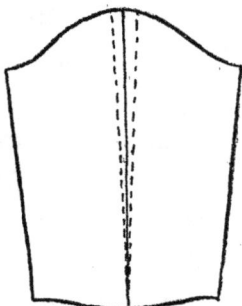

FIG. 73

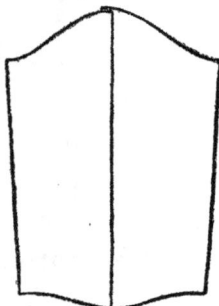

FIG. 74

See Fig. 73. From these points run diagonal lines to the center of the sleeve at the bottom.

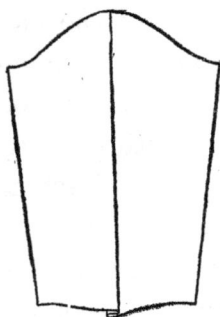

FIG. 75

Crease along one of the diagonal lines and fold it over to the other to form the tuck. See Fig. 74.

To Make a Sleeve Narrower from Top to Bottom. — Bring the side edges of the sleeve pattern together and crease through the center. Mark the amount to be taken out of the sleeve, half on one side of the center and

[84]

half on the other.   Crease along one of these marks and fold it over to the other.   See Fig. 75.

To Increase the Size of a Sleeve at the Top. — Bring the side edges of the sleeve pattern together and crease through the center.   Then cut the pattern along the crease. Mark a straight line on a plain piece of paper. Place half the pattern on one side of the line and half on the other.   Keep the lower edges even and touching the line.   Spread the pattern apart at the top the desired amount,

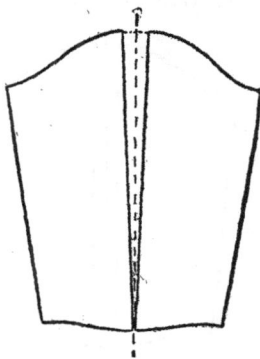

Fig. 76

keeping the two pieces equal distances from the line.   See Fig. 76.   Mark around the outline of the pieces and it will give a sleeve pattern of increased size at the top.

To Widen a Sleeve from Top to Bottom. — Split the pattern through the center and lay the two pieces either side of a straight line

[85]

marked on plain paper as described in the paragraph before. Keep the tops and bottoms even and move the pieces equal distances from the line. See Fig. 77. Mark around the pieces for a new pattern.

To Shorten a Sleeve. — Mark off the seam allowance at top, sides and bottom. Fold the sleeve crosswise bringing the bottom of

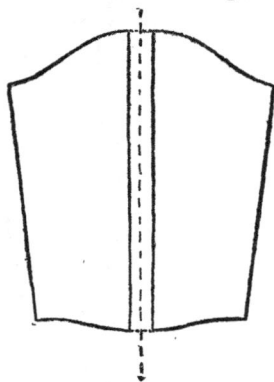

FIG. 77

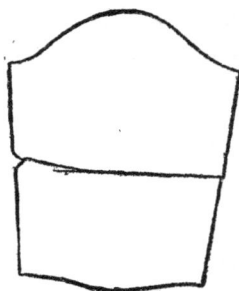

FIG. 78

the sleeve to the top and matching the corners at the bottom where the seams are marked off with the corners at the armhole where the seams are marked off. Crease through the center. Lay in a tuck the desired depth, taking up half the amount either side of the crease. See Fig. 78.

[86]

To Lengthen a Sleeve. — Fold crosswise as described above and mark exact center. Cut the sleeve pattern through the center. Mark a straight line on a plain piece of material. Lay one piece of the pattern above and one below the line. Keep the edges even and spread the pieces, moving both pieces the same distance from the line. See Fig. 79. Mark around the outside for a new pattern.

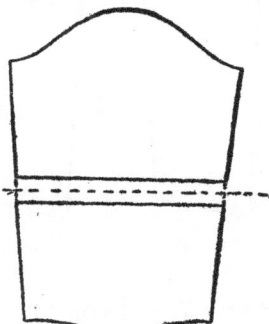

Fig. 79

Testing a Sleeve to See if it Will Twist. — Mark off the seam allowance on the pattern at the top, sides and bottom. Crease the sleeve pattern through the center, bringing side edges together. The edges at the sides should exactly match, both above and below the elbow when the center of the sleeve is folded in one straight continuous crease. See Fig. 80. If when the sleeve is creased and the edges matched above the elbow, the edges do not come together below the elbow,

[87]

the sleeve will twist. See Fig. 81. In this case, true up the sleeve pattern by cutting off a trifle on one edge below the elbow and adding to the other until they exactly match.

FIG. 80   FIG. 81

Adding Reach Room to a Sleeve. — If sleeves draw when the arms are brought foreward, the strain coming across the back from elbow to elbow there is not reach room enough in the sleeves. Before using the pattern again, trace off the seams, lay the pattern on another piece of paper and add a little more goods to the top of the pattern at the side back. See Fig. 82. This lengthens the sleeve at just the point where the strain comes.

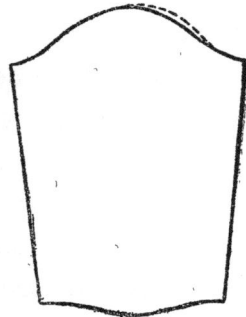

FIG. 82

[88]

Shirt Sleeves. — These are cut the same front and back and the seam in the sleeve matches the underarm seam. Shirt sleeves should be sewed to the armhole before the sleeve or underarm seams are closed. Pin the sleeve to the armhole, working from the wrong side of the garment and with the sleeve toward you. Ease the sleeve to the armhole at all points. See Fig. 83. Double stitch the sleeve to the armhole, turning the raw

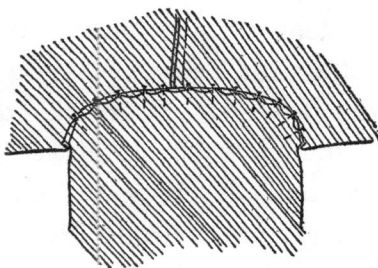

FIG. 83

edges into the garment. See *Double Stitched Seams*, page 33. After the sleeve is sewed to the armhole, close the sleeve and underarm seam in one continuous stitching.

Waist Sleeves Having Seams Matching Underarm Seams. — In this case, too, the sleeve should be sewed to the armhole before the sleeve and underarm seams are closed.

Pin the sleeve to the armhole, easing it to the armhole at the side front and side back, and pinning it plain to the armhole at the top and bottom. These sleeves are sometimes French seamed, sometimes double stitched, and sometimes plain seamed and bound. See *Seams,* page 31 and *Binding,* page 113.

Sleeves with Seams that do not Match Underarm Seams. — Here the underarm and the sleeve seams are closed before the sleeve is joined to the armhole. Pin the sleeve to the armhole, working from the wrong side of the garment. Ease the sleeve to the armhole at the side front and back, and pin it to the armhole plain at the top and underarm. Baste both sleeves to the garment. If the garment fitted smoothly before the sleeves were sewed in, then, after the sleeves are basted in, draws either through the body portion or in the sleeve, you will know that the fault is in the sleeves. Rip them out and shift them to the front or the back until the garment fits smoothly and the arms can be moved with freedom. The best finish is obtained in this type of sleeve by plain stitching it to the armhole and then binding the armhole.

Sleeves with Fullness at the Top. — Sleeves of this type are usually made with seams that do not match the underarm seams. Join the underarm and sleeve seams before joining the sleeve to the armhole. Run a gather thread all the way around the sleeve. Pin the sleeve to the armhole, working from the wrong side of the garment. Place most of the fullness at the top, side front and back, but ease the sleeve slightly to the armhole at all points.

For *Coat Sleeves*, see page 132.

CHAPTER VIII

FINISHING

Darts. — When a triangular-shaped piece of material is taken up to eliminate fullness it forms a dart. In forming a dart mark the amount of material to be taken up and where the dart will end. Crease the material centerway between the marks, bringing the right sides of the goods together, and stitch the dart. Curve the stitching, reversing the curve at the top and gradually running it off to nothing. See Fig. 84. It gives a well-rounded, smooth dart on the right side of the goods. If the dart is stitched straight across, it will end in a blunt point which will poke out on the right side of the garment.

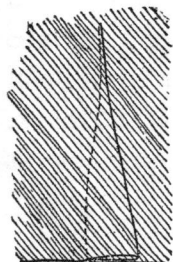

Fɪɢ. 84

Facings. — *A straight facing* is formed by sewing a straight piece of material to a raw

edge and turning it back on the wrong side.
Lay the facing piece along the edge to be
faced, with the right sides of the
material together. Stitch the
length of the facing. Turn the
facing onto the wrong side of
the garment, fold under the raw
edge a seam's width, press and stitch
the facing to the material, running
the stitching along the folded
edge of the facing. See Fig. 85.

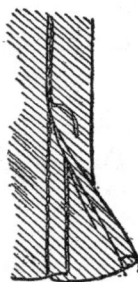

FIG. 85

A *shaped facing* is one which faces a curved
or pointed edge and is cut the same shape as
the outside piece. Use the pattern as a guide

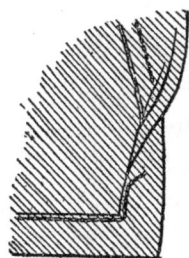

in cutting the facing, marking
back on the edge of the pattern the width of the facing
plus seams. This gives a pattern for the facing. Stitch the
facing to the garment in the
same manner as a straight
facing. See Fig. 86.

FIG. 86

Casings. — An extra piece of material applied to a garment, for the purpose of carry-

ing an elastic or draw string, is called a casing. The waistlines of children's guimpes, ladies' blouses and the tops of petticoats are finished in this manner.

When the casing is placed centerway of a piece, cut a strip of material one inch wide. Turn under the ends and stitch across them. Mark where the lower edge of the casing will

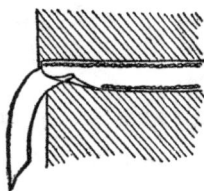

FIG. 87

come on the material. Lay the casing on the wrong side of the garment below the mark, with only a seam allowance lapping over the mark. Stitch the casing to the garment, running the stitching a seam's width in from the edge. Fold the casing over. Turn under the free edge a seam's width and stitch it flat to the garment. Insert elastic, fastening it to the garment at either end with over and over stitches, or insert a draw string. See Fig. 87.

To make a casing at the edge of a piece, cut material for casing and finish ends as described above. Join casing to lower edge the same as a facing, see *Facing,* page 92, then insert elastic or a draw string.

To Miter Corners. — In order to turn a corner in a straight piece of material, it is necessary to take a V-shaped dart. This forms a mitered corner.

Lay the straight strip of material face down on a smooth surface. Determine where the corner is to be and swing the material around until the outer edges lie in the desired position. Pinch up the surplus goods at the corner until the material is smooth. Pin the dart thus formed and stitch across it. See Fig. 88. Cut off the material in the dart, leaving only a narrow seam. Turn the piece right side out, fold the raw edges of the seam to one side of the miter and stitch across the mitered corner again.

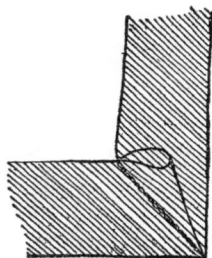

FIG. 88

Lining Trimming Pieces. — The lining for any trimming piece should be cut a trifle smaller than the outside. Otherwise the lining will wrinkle and bulge beyond the outside of the piece.

Use the pattern for the outside trimming piece as a guide in cutting the lining, cutting the lining one eighth of an inch smaller on all edges than the outside. Lay the lining on the outside piece, with the right sides of the material together and baste around the edges,

FIG. 89

keeping the edges of the two pieces exactly even by holding the outside to the lining at all points. Stitch around the outside edges, leaving a space open for two inches in order to turn the trimming piece right side out. Cut the seam off diagonally at the corners to avoid bulk. Turn the trimming piece right side out, fold under the free edges a seam's width and blind stitch across the opening. See *Blind Stitching*, page 22. The edge of the trimming piece will be thin and neat. See Fig. 89.

Yokes.—In children's dresses, ladies tailored blouses and men's shirts, yokes are usually lined.

To make a lined yoke, cut the lining the same shape as the outside yoke. In joining, insert the material which comes below the yoke between the yoke and the yoke lining. To do this, lay the yoke on top of the piece which is to be joined to it, with the face side of the yoke next to the face side of the material and the lower edge of the yoke even with

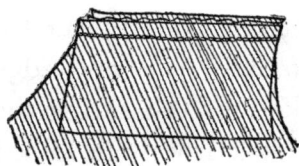

FIG. 90

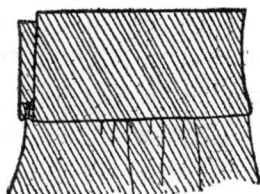

FIG. 91

the upper edge of lower piece. Baste in position and place the yoke lining on the wrong side of the lower piece in a position corresponding to the position of the outside yoke. Stitch across the three pieces. See Fig. 90. Turn the yoke and the yoke lining up into their finished position and press. See Fig. 91. From the right side of the garment, stitch across the yoke again, running the stitching above the first joining.

[97]

Unlined yokes are double stitched to the piece below. See *Double Stitched Seams,* page 33.

Yokes with tucks at the lower edge are lapped over the piece which comes below and stitched like a tuck. To finish a yoke of this type fold back the lower edge a seam's width more than the width of the finished tuck. Press this edge. Lap the bottom of the yoke over the lower piece, keeping the upper edge of the lower piece even with the raw edge folded under on the yoke. Stitch across the yoke, the tuck's width back from the folded edge.

Collars. — *Detachable soft shirt collars* are usually interlined. Use a coarse lawn or linen for the interlining. Make the interlining one, two or three thicknesses according to the desired stiffness of the collar.

Use the collar pattern as a guide in cutting the interlining, cutting off the seams at the outer edges. Cut two pieces for the outside collar. Lay the interlining on the wrong side of the under collar piece and baste in

[98]

place. Place the top collar on the under
collar with the right sides of the material together. Stitch around the outside edges,
being careful not to catch the interlining in
the seam. Leave a two-inch opening at the
lower edge of the collar for turning the collar
right side out. To avoid bulkiness at the
edges cut off the seam near the stitching.
Turn the collar right side out. Turn under
the raw edges at the opening and blind stitch
across the opening by hand. See *Blind
Stitching*, page 22. Stitch around the outside of the collar again, running the stitching
any desired distance from the edge.

Collars which are lined should have the lining cut smaller than the outside. See *Lining
Trimming Pieces*, page 95. Leave the neck
edges of the lining and the collar raw.

Collars which are hemmed must be cut
straight at the edges. It is impossible to turn
a neat hem on a curved edge. Turn the hem
first onto the right side of the garment. At
the corners pinch out the surplus goods, and
stitch across diagonally. See *To Miter Cor-*

ners, page 95. Then fold the hem onto the wrong side, turn under the free edges a seam's width, and press the edges. Stitch around the collar, working from the right side of the collar and running the stitching a hem's width from the edge.

Collars which are faced give the same appearance as hemmed collars. Square collars can be finished with a straight facing. See *Straight Facings,* page 92. In this case the corners should be mitered. See *To Miter Corners,* page 95. The best result is obtained in round or fancy-shaped collars when a shaped facing is used. See *Shaped Facings,* page 93.

Finishing the Neck. — As soon as the shoulder seams are closed in any garment, run a thread around the neck by hand and draw up the material slightly. This is to prevent stretching.

Collar bands are used as a finish at the neck where the garment has a detachable collar, as in the case of shirts and some tailored blouses. Cut two pieces for the collar band. Lay the two pieces of the band with the right sides of the material together. Stitch the two pieces together, running the stitching a seam's width in from the edge at the ends and across the top. To avoid bulk, cut the seams away close to the stitching. Turn the band right side out and press. Mark the center-front and center-back on the band.

Place the band on the wrong side of the garment, with the raw edges of the band even with the neck edge of the garment. Keep the center-front and center-back of the band even with the center-front and center-back of the

FIG. 92

garment. Stitch the edge of the band which comes next to the garment to the neck edge of the garment. Turn the band up into the finished position, fold in the raw edge a seam's width, and stitch this free edge over the raw edges on the right side of the garment. See Fig. 92.

If the collar is lined, place the collar on the wrong side of the garment with the right side of the collar next to the wrong side of the garment and the raw edges on the collar even with the neck edge of the garment. Stitch the edge of the collar which comes next to the garment to the neck edge of the garment. Turn the collar onto the right side of the garment, fold under the free edge a seam's width and stitch this edge over the raw edges or fell it down by hand. See Fig. 93. See *Felling*, page 22.

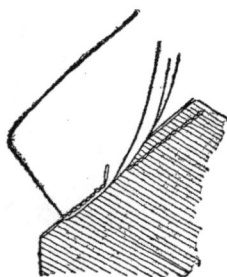

Fig. 93

If the collar is faced or hemmed finish the neck of the garment in sewing on the collar with a narrow facing. Cut the facing bias, three quarters of an inch wide. See *Cutting True Bias*, page 18.

Lay the collar on the right side of the garment, with the wrong side of the collar next to the right side of the garment and the edges even at the neck. Place the facing along the neck edge and stitch around the

[102]

neck. To avoid bulk, cut the seam off close to the stitching. Turn the facing onto the wrong side of the garment. Fold under the ends and raw edge. Fell the facing in place, see *Felling*, page 22, or stitch it down by machine. See Fig. 94.

If the front of the waist has revers, join the under collar to the neck edge of the waist, with the raw edges of the seam extending on the inside of the waist. The front of the waist should have facings. Use the front of the pattern as a guide in cutting these. The upper portion of the facing

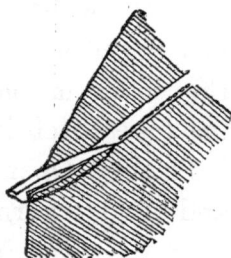

FIG. 94

should extend two inches beyond the roll line of the revers. Join the upper edge of the facings to the neck edge of the collar. The raw edge of the seam should extend on the wrong side. Then join the collar and front facings to the waist. Place the facings and collar on the right side of the garment, keeping edges even. Stitch around the out-

[103]

side edges of the collar and down the fronts. Cut the seams off diagonally at the corners to avoid clumsiness. Turn the collar and facings onto the wrong side of the garment. Turn under the raw edges a seam's width and stitch in place or turn off a seam's width on the back edge of the front facing and stitch along the fold, leaving the facing free from the waist. In this case, turn under the raw edges at the neck of the collar and fell the collar in place, see *Felling*, page 22, or machine stitch it down.

Slashed Openings at the Neck. — Middies and similar garments which slip on over the head have the front slashed at the neck. A slash of this type is finished with a facing. Do not slash the material until the facing is stitched in place.

Where the collar extends to the center-front, the slash is faced before the collar is joined to the neck. Cut the facing to extend two inches beyond the slash at all points. Turn a narrow hem on the outer edges of the facing or bind these edges. See *Binding*, page 113.

Mark where the slash is to be placed on the front of the garment. Cover this mark with the facing piece, placing the facing piece on the right side of the material and centerway over the mark. Mark the slash on the facing piece. Stitch either side of the mark, placing the stitching one eighth of an inch from the mark at the top and running the stitching to a point below the mark. See Fig. 95. Slash centerway between the stitching and turn the facing onto the wrong side of the garment. Stitch the outer edges of the facing to the garment, or let the facing hang free. Work eyelets either side of the slash and fasten with a lace. Join the collar to the neck edge in the regular way. See *Collars*, page 98.

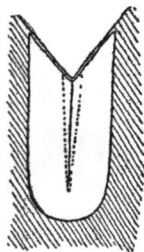

FIG. 95

Where the front of the garment turns back in revers, face the slash as described above. In joining the collar to the neck edge stitch the under collar to the neck edge of the garment, and the under side of the revers and the top

collar to the revers facing. Fell the raw
edges of the collar over the raw edges of the
garment at the back of the neck.

Waistbands. — Cut the waistband to correspond to the waist measure, allowing laps
and seams at the ends. It should be twice
the desired finished width plus seams. Fold
the waistband through the center with the
right sides together and
stitch across the ends.
Turn the waistband right
side out, fold under the
lower edges a seam's width
and press. Mark the cen-
ter-front and back on both the waistband
and the garment. Insert the raw edge of
the garment between the two thicknesses of
the waistband, keep the center-fronts and
backs even, and stitch. See Fig. 96.

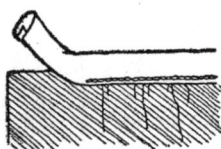

Fig. 96

Inside Belts of Grosgrain Belting. — *Raised
waistline skirts* are sometimes hung from the
top of an inside belt of stiff grosgrain webbing.
The webbing should measure just the amount
the skirt is cut above the normal waistline.

The inside belt should correspond to the waist measure and have hems allowed at the ends. The ends of the belt should just come together, after the hems are turned, and be finished with hooks and eyes. Mark the center-front and center-back on the belt.

After the gores of the skirt have been joined and the placket finished, join to the top of the inside belt, bringing the center-front and back of the skirt to the center-front and back of the belt. Working from the right side of the skirt, lap the top of the skirt a seam's width over the edge of the belt, with the belt extending straight up above the skirt. Baste the skirt in this position, turn down the belt inside the skirt and try on the skirt to see if it needs readjustment. In stitching the skirt to the belt, turn the belt up above the skirt, as it was first. Stitch through one thickness of the skirt and the belt. Cover the raw edge with a fold of material or tape and stitch the tape or material along either side. Then turn the belt down into the skirt. The top of the skirt will roll over the top of the belt and give a clean finish. See Fig. 97.

One-piece dresses often have grosgrain belting as a stay at the waistline. Finish off the waist portion of the garment except at the lower edge. Join the skirt gores, and finish the placket and lay in any pleats, or gather any fullness at the top.

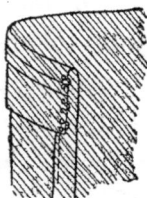

FIG. 97

If the dress is made with a raised waistline, make the belt tight enough so the lower edges will stay at the normal waistline and the belt extend above. Finish the ends of the belt with hems and hooks and eyes, and mark the center-front and back on the belt. Try on the belt and adjust the lower edge of the waist over the top of the belt, bringing the center-front and back of the waist to these points in the belt. Put the skirt on over the waist and belt, turn under the top of the skirt a seam's width, bring the center and back of the skirt to these points in the waist and belt, and pin securely to the belt. Re-

[108]

move the garment and stitch through the skirt, the waist and the belt, running the stitching along the top of the belt.

If the dress is normal waistline, make the belt a trifle looser so the center will stay at the normal waistline. In adjusting the waist and skirt to the belt, stitch along the center of the belt.

Hemming the Bottom of Skirts. — *Straight skirts* should have the hems turned evenly all the way around, and any adjusting should be done from the top. Before turning the hem bind the edge, see *Binding,* page 113, or fold under a seam's width and stitch along the edge of the fold. Turn the hem, press it and stitch by machine or fell by hand. See *Felling,* page 22.

In circular skirts there is fullness at the top of the hem. After the hem has been turned back, run a gather thread around the top of the hem, drawing it up so it is just the size of the skirt. The fullness should run straight down at all points. In woolen materials or cottons in woolen finish, shrink out some of the fullness at the top of the hem. See *To Steam Out Slight Ease or Fullness*, page 18. Bind the top of the hem and fell by hand or machine stitch.

The Top of Boys' Trousers. — The edges are faced and finished with a button band. Cut strips of material for bands wide enough

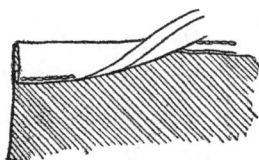 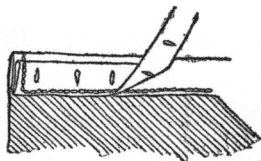

FIG. 98   FIG. 99

to be folded double, one for front and one for back of trousers, and long enough to reach across. Fold bands through center, turn under raw edges, press and stitch around them. Face front and back of trousers. See Fig. 98 and *Facings*, page 47. Work buttonholes in bands and stitch lower edges of bands to trousers, keeping top of bands even with top of trousers. See Fig. 99. Buttonholes in band should match buttons on under waist.

CHAPTER IX

TRIMMING

Bound Buttonholes. — The neatest and strongest buttonhole is made by facing the slash with one piece of material, turned at either side of the slash to give the appearance of binding. Mark where the buttonhole is to be placed on the face side of the material. Cover the mark with a facing piece, cut to extend one-half inch beyond the mark at all points. Mark the buttonhole on the facing

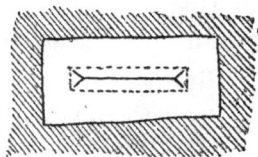

FIG. 100

piece. Stitch either side of the mark and square across the ends, running the stitching one eighth of an inch from the mark at all points. Slash centerway between the stitchings to within one eighth of an inch of the end. From these points slash diagonally to the corners. See Fig. 100. Turn the facing through

[111]

the slash onto the wrong side. At the ends
of the buttonhole the facing will fall into
two small pleats. Stitch across the ends of
the buttonhole again, stitching the facing to

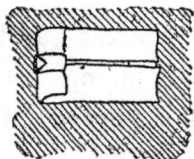

FIG. 101

the triangular portion which
was formed by slashing diagonally to the corners. See Fig.
101. Turn under the raw edges
of the facing, and fell by hand,
see *Felling*, page 22, or baste

it in place and, working from the right side
of the garment, stitch around the buttonhole
again. See Fig. 102.

Piping. — A piping is a bias fold inserted
under the edge of a piece or in
the seam. Cut material for
piping in one-inch bias strips.
See *Cutting Bias*, page 18. Join
the strips, taking a narrow
seam and press the raw edges of the seam
open.

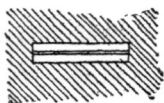

FIG. 102

If the edge of a garment is to be piped fold
over one edge of the piping a quarter of an
inch, and press. Turn back the other edge

an eighth of an inch and stitch near this edge.
Turn under the edge to be piped a seam's
width and press. Place the piping under this
edge with the edge of the piping extending one
eighth of an inch beyond the piece. See
Fig. 103. Stitch from the
right side of the garment.

If a seam is to be piped,
fold the piping through the
center, bringing the wrong
sides together, and press.
Turn under the edge of one
piece to be joined a seam's

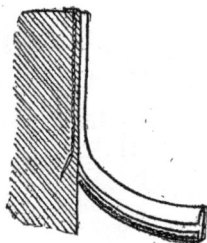

Fig. 103

width. Place the piping under this edge
with the edge of the piping extending one
eighth of an inch beyond the piece, and baste
in place. Lap the piece thus piped, over the
piece it is to join to, the width of a seam.
Stitch through the two pieces and the piping, running the stitching along the edge of
the upper piece. Bind or overcast the raw
edges on the wrong side of the garment.

Binding. — Edges which are to be bound
should have the seam allowance cut off of

them. A binding is stitched one side of the material, rolled over the edge and stitched to the other side. It neither adds to nor takes away from the size of a piece. Cut the material for binding bias one and one eighth inches wide. See *Cutting True Bias*, page 18. Join the strips, taking a narrow seam, and press the raw edges of the seams open. Lay the binding along the edge of the material with the right side of the binding next to the wrong side of the goods. Stitch along the edge, running the stitching one quarter of an inch from the edge. Fold the binding over onto the right side of the goods. Turn under the free edge of the binding one quarter of an inch and stitch the binding flat to the material. See Fig. 104.

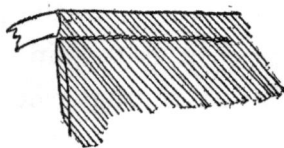

FIG. 104

FIG. 105

Cording. — This trimming is formed by rolling the material over a cord and catching it just in back of the cord. Cotton cable cord comes in various widths for this purpose. See Fig. 105.

Air Cording. — In heavy materials pin tucks are called air cording. The narrow tuck ridges up the material like a cording. See *Pin Tucks*, page 38.

Hemstitching with an Ordinary Sewing Machine. — Seams can be stitched to simulate hemstitching by inserting blotting paper between the two thicknesses of the goods. Lay the two pieces to be joined with the face sides of the material together and the edges

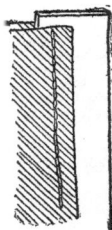 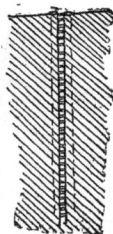

FIG. 106   FIG. 107

even. Insert strips of blotting paper between the two pieces at the edge. See Fig. 106. Remove the sewing machine foot, loosen the tensions and stitch through the two thicknesses of the material and the blotting paper. Tear the paper away, turn the raw edges of the seams away from each other and stitch either side of the seam. See Fig. 107. The hemstitching can be widened by using two or three thicknesses of blotting paper.

Lace Insertion. — The easiest way to handle lace insertion is to apply it to the top of the material, then cut the material away underneath. Baste the insertion in the desired position. Stitch either side of the insertion. Cut the material underneath,

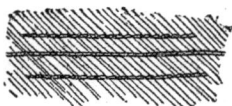

FIG. 108

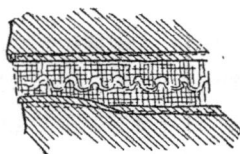

FIG. 109

leaving only a narrow seam allowance on either side. See Fig. 108. Fold back the raw edges on the wrong side and stitch either side of the insertion again, this time catching down the raw edges. See Fig. 109.

Lace Edging. — The best result is obtained by sewing the lace to the top of the material. If the lace is gathered, draw it up on the cord at the top. Lay this edge a seam's width in from the edge of the material. Stitch along the inside edge of the lace. Turn the raw edge of the material back and stitch along the inside edge of the lace again to catch the material in place. On the wrong side, cut off the raw edge close to the stitching. See Fig. 110.

FIG. 110

CHAPTER X

BE YOUR OWN DESIGNER

How to Use a Block Waist Pattern. — A plain waist pattern can be used as a basis for working out new designs. Use a plain high neck waist pattern without tucks or fullness. Cut off the seam allowances. Seams are confusing when working out a new design.

To add a yoke. Pencil the outline of the yoke on the pattern. See Fig. 111. Lay the pattern on another piece of paper. Mark around the upper portion of the pattern, and run a tracing wheel across the lower line of the yoke. Remove the pattern, and add seams beyond the marks at all points. Make a pattern for the lower portion by marking around the outside lower lines and trace across the yoke line, adding seams.

FIG. 111

To put in fullness below the yoke draw lines every two inches apart parallel to the center-front if it is the front of the waist, or parallel to the center-back if it is the back of the waist. Split the pattern along these lines and spread the pieces, keeping the edges parallel. Start with the piece nearest the center-front if it is the front of the waist, or center-back if it is the back of the waist. Square a line out at right angles from the top of this piece. Place the next piece with the top touching the line squared out from

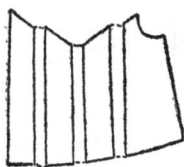

FIG. 112

the first piece. Square a line out from the second piece in the same manner and place the top of the third piece on this line. Place the rest of the pieces in the same manner. See Fig. 112. Mark around the outside edges. Remove the pattern. Draw straight lines from the highest to the lowest point on the yoke edge and smooth the curve at the bottom of the waist. Add seams at all points.

To add fullness at the top of the piece only, mark lines two inches apart on the pattern and split it into narrow pieces, but spread the pieces at the top only. Thumb tack the pieces so they just touch at the bottom, and spread them at the top. Mark around the outside edges, remove the pieces and draw new lines touching the highest and lowest points. Add seams.

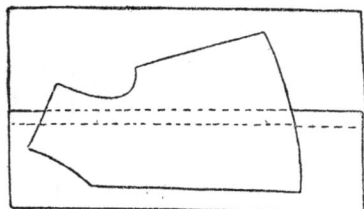

FIG. 113

To add tucks, mark where the tuck will come on the pattern. Lay the pattern on a plain piece of paper. Mark around the front portion as far as the tuck if it is the front pattern, or around the back portion as far as the tuck if it is the back pattern. Remove the pattern and lay in the tuck. Then lay on the pattern again and mark the rest of the outline. See Fig. 113. Add seams to pattern and cut piece while tuck is folded in place.

[120]

For groups of narrow tucking, spread the pattern as for fullness, see *To Add Fullness,* page 119, or tuck the material, then lay on the plain pattern and cut out the piece, allowing seams.

To add a hem, allow half the depth of the hem beyond the edge of the pattern, then the width of the hem plus a seam to turn back. This allows for a lap at the closing.

To take out the fullness at the bottom of the waist fit it out in darts, split the pattern at the armhole or lay in pleats at the under-arm seam.

There are two kinds of darts, those from the bust to the bottom and those at the shoulder. To locate darts below bust, cut pattern in cheap material and try on, pinning up darts to fit the figure. For a dart at the shoulder, mark a line centerway through the shoulder, following the slant of the shoulder, then running parallel to the center-front down to the bottom of the pattern. Lap out the desired amount of material below the bust which will spread the pattern

at the shoulder. Mark around the piece, indicating dart, and add seams. See Fig. 114.

Fig. 114

Another way to take out the
fullness is to spread the armhole.
Slash the pattern parallel to
center-front. On a level with
the bust line, slash over to the
armhole. Keep the pattern together at the bust line, lap the
lower edge and spread the armhole. See Fig. 115. Of course
this enlarges the armhole a trifle. Trace
around the outside of the pattern, smooth
up the curve at the armhole,
and add seams.

The fullness can also be taken
out at the underarm. In this
case, slash the pattern parallel
to center-front to the bust line.
From the top of this slash run
three slashes to the underarm
seam. Keep the pieces together
at the bust line. Lap the pieces at the lower
edge which will spread the pieces at the

Fig. 115

underarm. Mark around the outside of the
pattern and add seams. See Fig. 116. In
making the garment take up the
amount spread at the underarm
in pleats.

Position of lace or insertion
should first be indicated on the
block pattern. Pencil on where
the center of the lace or insertion
is to go. Then mark the finished
edge of the lace or insertion. See

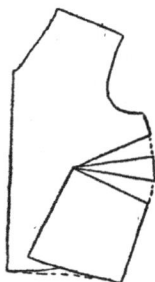

FIG. 116

Fig. 117. Lay the pattern on the goods and
run over these marks with a tracing wheel.

To sew on lace or insertion,
see *Lace* or *Insertion*, page 116.

**How to Use Block Skirt Pat-
tern.** — A seven-gored skirt of
normal waistline, without seams,
makes the best block pattern.

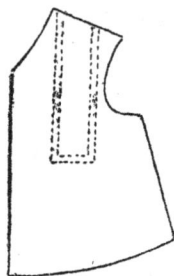

FIG. 117

To make fewer gores, place
the pattern on another piece
of paper. Lay the lower por-
tion of the gores along side of each other,
mark around the outside of the pieces and

[123]

the darts thus formed. See Fig. 118. Divide this pattern into as many pieces as
desired, marking
darts at the seams
which will equal the
darts taken out origi-
nally. See Fig. 119.
Lay this diagram
over another piece
of paper and run a
tracing wheel around
the outline of the new gore. Remove the
pattern, add seams and cut out. To make
the skirt smaller at
the bottom, lap the
gores as indicated in
Fig. 120.

*If the skirt is to
have raised waist line,*
measure around the
body where the top
of the skirt will
come. Lay the gores on a plain piece of
paper, mark the position of the new waist-

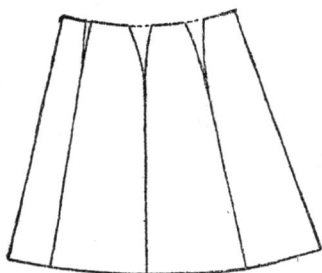
Fig. 118

Fig. 119

line above each gore, and add sufficient to either side of the gores to equal the new waist measurement. If the skirt is to have a fitted appearance at the top, run the lines from the top of each gore to the old normal waist-line. See Fig. 121. If the skirt is to hang

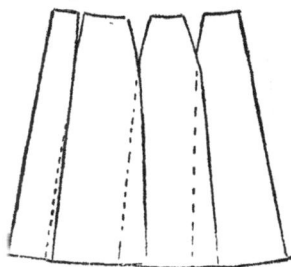

FIG. 120

straight from the raised waistline to the hips, draw a straight line from the top of each gore to the hip. See Fig. 122.

FIG. 121

FIG. 122

Add pleats to a skirt in the same way as adding tucks to a waist. See *To Add Tucks,* page 120. *To add a group of pleats coming only part way on a skirt,* mark on the plain gore the outline the gore will take and the exact position of the pleats. See Fig. 123. Lay the pattern on another piece of material,

[125]

trace the outside edges and the new outline along what will be the folded edge of the

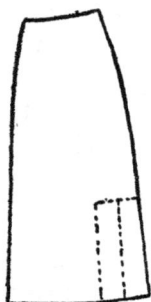

FIG. 123   FIG. 124

first pleat. Add seams at the outer edges and add the width of the pleat plus a seam beyond the fold edge of the pleat. See Fig. 124. Slash the pattern where the pleat turns back, and fold the pleat back before cutting out the bottom of the gore. Cut out the pleated section in the old pattern and use it as a guide for cutting the new pattern with the pleats on. See Fig. 125. Follow the same method in laying in the pleat as in laying in tucks in a

FIG. 125   FIG. 126

waist. Cut an extension on the gore which is to join to the pleated section. See Fig. 126,

[126]

To determine the size of pleats in a straight side-pleated skirt, decide on the number of widths to be put in the skirt, join the pieces, measure the top of the skirt and the waist-line of the figure. The difference between the waist measure and the top of the skirt will give the amount of material to be taken out in the pleats. Divide this equally by the number of pleats and it will give the amount to be taken up in each pleat. To space the pleats, decide how wide you want the space at center-front, subtract this amount from the waist measure. Then divide the remaining waist measure by one less than the number of pleats. This gives the width of the spaces between the pleats.

How to Hang Your Own Skirt. — Finish off the waistline of the skirt and try it on. Stand near a table which comes about fifteen inches below the waistline. Place pins in the skirt where the table touches the skirt. Turn up the skirt at the center-front the desired amount. Remove the skirt and

make the distance from the pins to the
lower edge the same at all points. As the
curve of the hips comes above the table any
differences in the length will be from the
pin to the top.

CHAPTER XI

COAT MAKING

Shrink the Materials. — Woolens and cottons cannot be properly worked up and pressed unless they are first shrunk. The canvas for interlining should also be thoroughly shrunk before it is cut. See *Shrinking Material,* page 9.

Canvasing the Front. — The fronts of a cloth coat need reinforcement so the coat will hold to shape and set smoothly. Use tailor's canvas. Use the pattern for the front of the coat

Fig. 127

as a guide in cutting the canvas. The canvas should cover the coat above the bust line, while in the lower portion it should face back the front edge for a distance of six inches. See Fig. 127. Cut the seam off the neck, front and lower edge of the canvas.

[129]

Place the canvas on the wrong side of the front, a seam's width back from the edge. Baste it securely to position. If the front of the coat has a lapel, catch the canvas to the lapel with padding stitches. See *Padding Stitches*, page 23.

Taping the Edges. — To prevent stretching, tape the front edge of the coat. Use thin linen tape about one quarter of an inch wide. Lay the tape on the canvas, and catch the tape to the canvas and outside material, taking a stitch first on one side and then on the other. At all points hold the outside material and canvas into the tape. See Fig. 128. Run the tape at the neck edge, along the roll line of the lapel and down the front. After the shoulder seams are joined tape the back of the coat at the neck.

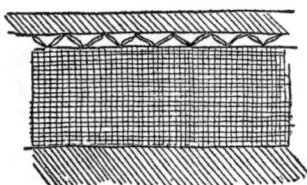

FIG. 128

The Collar. — An interlining of tailor's canvas is needed for the collar. Use the col-

lar pattern as a guide in cutting the canvas,
cutting off the seam allowance at the outer
edge. Baste the canvas to the under collar.
If the collar is a tailored notched collar,
cover the stand (crescent-shaped portion
which comes next to the neck) with rows of
machine stitching. See Fig. 129. Catch the
canvas to the rest of the collar with padding

stitches. In soft rolling
collars catch the canvas
to the entire collar with
padding stitches.

FIG. 129

**Joining the Collar and Front Facings to
the Coat.** — After the front of the coat has
been canvased and taped and the shoulder
and underarm seams closed, join the under
collar, reinforced with the canvas, to the
neck. Press the raw edges of the seam down
onto the coat. Join the top collar to the
facing. Then lay the top collar and facing
on the outside of the coat, along the front
of the coat, and the under side of the collar.
Stitch around the outside edges and turn
the collar into its finished position, and the

facing onto the wrong side of the coat.
Draw the facing back at the edge until the
seam is on the wrong side of
the garment. Baste into position and press. See Fig. 130.

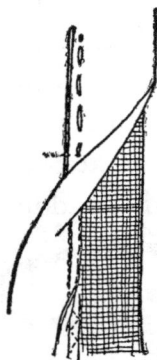

FIG. 130

Staying the Lower Edge. —
To prevent the lower edge from
stretching, reinforce it with inch-
wide strips of tailor's canvas.
Lay the lower edge of the canvas along the line where the
bottom of the coat will turn
up. Catch the canvas to the
material, taking a stitch, first on one side
and then on the other. Use care that the
stitches do not show through onto the right
side of the goods. Turn the lower edge up
on the canvas.
Press and catch
it into place. See
Fig. 131.

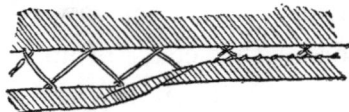

FIG. 131

The Sleeve. — Regulation coat sleeves are
made in two pieces, the top sleeve having
slight fullness at the elbow.

[132]

Sleeves with vents at the back seam should have the vents finished before the back seams are closed. Stay the lower edge with an inch-wide strip of canvas, caught first on one side and then on the other. See Fig. 132. Usually there is an extension cut on the under sleeve at the vent. Face the lower edge of the sleeve all the way across, letting the facing extend above the vent. See *Facing*, page 92. Close the back seam and press the seams open. Shrink out the fullness at the elbow of the upper sleeve. See *Steaming Out Ease or Fullness*, page 18.

FIG. 132

Sleeves without vents have the back seams closed first. They are stitched all the way to the bottom. In this case there should be an extension cut on the bottom of the sleeve. Stay the bottom of the sleeve with a strip of canvas, then turn up the lower edge of the sleeve on the canvas and catch it in place.

Sleeves with cuffs have the seams closed as described in sleeves without vents. The

[133]

neatest finish is obtained when the seam is cut off the lower edge of the sleeve. Stay the bottom with canvas. The cuff should be cut with an extension to turn back onto the wrong side of the sleeve. Reinforce the cuff with an interlining of tailor's canvas. The canvas interlining should be cut without a seam at the top and without the lower extension. Close the seams in the outside cuff and lining. Baste the interlining to the outside cuff, lapping the edges flat at the seam, and join the cuff lining to the top of the cuff. Adjust the cuff to the lower edge of the sleeve, tacking the cuff lining to the sleeve. Roll the extension at the lower edge of the cuff onto the wrong side of the sleeve and catch it to the canvas.

Use the sleeve pattern as a guide *to cut the sleeve lining.* Join the seams in the lining and press them open. Turn the sleeve wrong side out and slip the lining over it. Tack the lining to the sleeve along the seams. Turn under the lower edge of the lining and fell it over the raw edges at the bottom of the sleeve. See *Felling*, page 22, and Fig. 133.

Sew the outside sleeve to the armhole. The sleeve lining is left free until the coat lining is put in. Pin the sleeve to the armhole, so that it hangs in the position the arm naturally hangs in. Baste it in place and try on the coat. If it draws, shift it to the front or back until the arm can be moved with freedom.

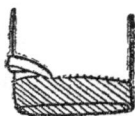

FIG. 133

Lining a Coat. — Use the coat pattern as a guide in cutting the lining. Allow a pleat at the center-back. This is to prevent the lining from drawing across the back. Join the seams in the lining and pin the lining to the coat. Smooth out all wrinkles and tack the lining to the coat at the underarm and shoulder seams. Baste it in place around the armhole. Turn under the edges of the lining and pin the lining over the raw edges of the coat at the neck, along the back edge of the front facing and at the bottom, placing the pins about an inch apart. Fell the lining in place. See *Felling*, page 22. After the coat lining is sewed in bring up the sleeve lining, turn under the edges and fell the sleeve lining over the raw edges at the armhole.

Unlined Coats. — If the coat is to be unlined, cut the cloth facing for the front to extend across to the armhole, above the bust line. Also cut a shoulder yoke for the back. Canvas and tape the coat as described before. Bind the lower edge of the back yoke and the outer edge of the front facing before joining to the coat. Join the back yoke to the front facing at the shoulder and fell the raw edges of the collar over the raw edges of the yoke at the back of the coat. Bind the raw edges of the underarm seams and the lower edge of the coat before turning it up. See *Binding*, page 113.

The Pressing is Important. — Press each piece before it is joined, each seam after it is joined, all edges and trimming pieces. It is impossible to properly press a coat after it is entirely made. See *Pressing*, page 18.

CHAPTER XII

FITTING

THE regulation size pattern is made to fit an average figure. It is made for a medium height of shoulder a medium length of waist, and for the figure which stands neither over erect nor stooping. If shoulders are sloping or square, if the waistline is short or long, if the figure is over erect or stooping, then changes are necessary in order to secure a perfect fit. Where there is any doubt as to the fit of a pattern, cut out a test garment in cheap muslin.

How to Fit Sloping Shoulders. — If the shoulders slope more than the average, wrinkles will appear diagonally from the neck to the underarm. To overcome this fault, take up the shoulder seam to conform to the slope of the shoulder. The seam should be taken up deepest at the armhole and only the seam allowance at the neck.

As this makes the armhole smaller, slash the material under the arm until the arm can be moved with freedom. Do not slash the armhole too deeply; the seam taken in sewing in the sleeve will enlarge it.

How to Fit Square Shoulders. — If shoulders are square the garment will wrinkle crosswise below the neck front and back. In this case take up the shoulder seam, fitting it deepest at the neck, while only the regulation seam is taken at the armhole. As this makes the neck smaller, slash the neck until the garment is comfortable.

If the Garment is Shortwaisted. — *In semi-fitted or fitted garments* the waistline can be made lower by taking up each seam a trifle at the point where the waistline should be.

If the Garment is Longwaisted. — When wrinkles appear crosswise above the waistline, the garment is too longwaisted. Take up the shoulder seams until the wrinkles disappear. Unless the shoulders are sloping

or square, the shoulder seams should be
taken up the same amount at all points.
This makes the armhole smaller. Slash
under the arms. If you know the pattern
is longwaisted, lay pleats in the pattern
pieces parallel to the waistline and sufficiently deep to take up the wrinkles before
cutting the goods.

If the Figure is Overly Erect. —When a
person stands with shoulders thrown back
and chest out and the garment was made for
a straight figure, then the garment will be
out of balance. It will poke out in front,
wrinkles will appear diagonally from the
bustline to the underarm and it will hang
away from the back of the neck. To secure
a perfect fit, it will be necessary to cut a
test in muslin; fit the garment, correct the
pattern and re-cut the pieces. Rip the underarm seams of the muslin and let the pieces
fall naturally, add a V-shaped piece at the
underarm and mark where the underarm
seam should come. This throws extra fullness in the front of the garment. Fit out

this fullness in the side-front seam. If the garment is made without a seam, split the piece parallel to the center-front up to the bustline, then across to the armhole. Keep the edges together at the bustline and lap onto the fullness at the lower edge. This enlarges the armhole a trifle.

If the Figure is Stooping. — When a person stoops or, in other words, the figure is tilted forward, and the pattern is made for a straight figure, then the garment will also be out of balance. This time wrinkles will appear at the back diagonally from the lower portion of the shoulder blades to the underarm, the garment will poke out in the back and is apt to bind at the back of the neck. To overcome these faults, cut a test in muslin, correct the muslin garment, make the same changes in the pattern, and re-cut the pieces. Rip the muslin at the underarm seams. Let the pieces fall into their natural position and insert a V-shaped portion at the underarm, re-marking where the underarm seam will come. Fit out the surplus goods at the bottom in the back seams, or if the back is one piece, dart out the extra goods at center-back in the pattern. Should this make the garment narrow across the back at the shoulders, add a trifle either side at the armhole.

Out Sizes. — If the chest is broad in proportion to the back or the back wide in proportion to the chest, buy two sizes of patterns, using one for the front and one for the back of the garment.

What Makes the Neck of a Garment Stand Away from the Figure. — When the neck of a garment bulges away from the form it is because it has been stretched. Rip off the collar, run a gather thread around the neck. Try on the garment and draw up the neck just enough so it lies close to the form. If care is used in distributing the fullness it will not be noticed after the collar is sewed on.

If the Front Edges of a Coat Hang Apart When the Coat is Unbottoned. — This may be caused by the garment being out of

[141]

balance. See *If the Figure is Stooping*, page
140. Another reason for it is that the front
edges are stretched. Remove the front facing and tape the edges, holding the material
into the tape. See *Taping*, page 130.

Skirts that Twist. — All seams of a skirt
should be stitched from the top down to
give the best hang. If one seam is stitched
upward and one down, the skirt is apt to
twist.

INDEX

INDEX

INDEX

INDEX

INDEX

INDEX

THERE is no royal road to learning.

IT is an old saying, and a true one, in a sense: for prince and peasant must alike travel the path.

YET, there are many paths, and great differences among them, as they lead to the temple of knowledge. In some, the going is easy: in some, hard. In some, the journeying is pleasant and profitable: in some, toilsome — a weary scramble over many stumbling blocks.

THE builder of the road is the teacher. It is his task to smooth the way, and to make it straight: or to leave it all cluttered, a twisted, haphazard course, that runs roughly and reaches nowhere.

IN the "Made Easy" Series, it has been the publisher's purpose to provide for the student the best possible road to learning — a road truly royal in its simplicity, its worth: a road wide and direct, and free from foolish, needless litter.

THE various writers of the books in the series have been chosen for their special fitness. Such fitness includes, in the first place, mastery of the particular subject: in the second place, ability to interpret knowledge to others.

RIGHT teaching makes easy learning. Few subjects are really hard to learn, when properly set before the pupil. These volumes are the product of a painstaking care to simplify every detail of instruction, yet to make it complete. The result for the student is, indeed, a learning made easy, yet none the less exact, thorough, wholly adequate for his needs.

The volumes now ready, or in the course of preparation — are:

Arithmetic Made Easy	Drawing Made Easy
Spelling Made Easy	Dressmaking Made Easy
Penmanship Made Easy	Dancing Made Easy
Grammar Made Easy	Etiquette Made Easy

Keeping Young Made Easy
Love Letters Made Easy
Shorthand Made Easy
Bookkeeping Made Easy
Entertaining Made Easy
Tricks and Magic Made Easy
Mental Healing Made Easy

Further titles will be added as opportunity presents itself to secure the proper type of manuscript.